IN MY OWN WORDS

Hay House Titles of Related Interest

YOU CAN HEAL YOUR LIFE, the movie,
starring Louise Hay & Friends
(available as a 1-DVD program and an expanded 2-DVD set)
Watch the trailer at: **www.LouiseHayMovie.com**

THE SHIFT, the movie,
starring Dr. Wayne W. Dyer
(available as a 1-DVD program and an expanded 2-DVD set)
Watch the trailer at: **www.DyerMovie.com**

ক্ষপ্পে

FOLLOWING SOUND INTO SILENCE:
Chanting Your Way Beyond Ego into Bliss (book-with-CD),
by Kurt (Kailash) A. Bruder, Ph.D., M.Ed.

THE GURU OF JOY: Sri Sri Ravi Shankar & the Art of Living,
by François Gautier

LIVING THE WISDOM OF THE TAO: The Complete
Tao Te Ching and Affirmations, by Dr. Wayne W. Dyer

PAST LIVES, PRESENT MIRACLES: The Most Empowering
Book on Reincarnation You'll Ever Read . . . in This Lifetime!
by Denise Linn

SECRETS OF THE LOST MODE OF PRAYER: The Hidden
Power of Beauty, Blessing, Wisdom, and Hurt, by Gregg Braden

YOUR SOUL'S COMPASS: What Is Spiritual Guidance?
by Joan Borysenko, Ph.D., and Gordon Dveirin, Ed.D.

ক্ষপ্পে

All of the above are available at your local
bookstore, or may be ordered by visiting:

Hay House USA: **www.hayhouse.com**®
Hay House Australia: **www.hayhouse.com.au**
Hay House UK: **www.hayhouse.co.uk**
Hay House South Africa: **www.hayhouse.co.za**
Hay House India: **www.hayhouse.co.in**

IN MY OWN WORDS

An Introduction to My
Teachings and Philosophy

HIS HOLINESS
THE DALAI LAMA

Edited by Rajiv Mehrotra

HAY HOUSE, INC.
Carlsbad, California • New York City
London • Sydney • Johannesburg
Vancouver • Hong Kong • New Delhi

Published and distributed in the United States by: Hay House, Inc.: www .hayhouse.com • *Published and distributed in Australia by:* Hay House Australia Pty. Ltd.: www.hayhouse.com.au • *Published and distributed in the United Kingdom by:* Hay House UK, Ltd.: www.hayhouse.co.uk • *Published and distributed in the Republic of South Africa by:* Hay House SA (Pty), Ltd.: www.hayhouse.co.za • *Distributed in Canada by:* Raincoast Books: www.raincoast.com • *Published in India by:* Hay House Publishers India: www.hayhouse.co.in

Editorial supervision: Jill Kramer • *Design:* Tricia Breidenthal

Library of Congress Control Number: 2008929371

Tradepaper ISBN: 978-1-4019-3184-1
Digital ISBN: 978-1-4019-2229-0

1st edition, September 2008
1st digital printing, January 2015

Printed in the United States of America

This book is dedicated
to all sentient beings
that we may be free
from our suffering and
to the great teachers
of all traditions
who teach us how.

CONTENTS

INTRODUCTION

The Foundation for Universal Responsibility of His Holiness The Dalai Lama (Tenzin Gyatso) is delighted, blessed, and honored to present this short introduction, in the words of His Holiness himself, to his ideas, teachings, and message for our fractured and troubled world.

Tenzin Gyatso, born of peasant parents, describes himself as "a simple Buddhist monk." He is celebrated by millions around the world for his profound insights into the human condition, why we experience suffering, and ways in which we can all find happiness. This is bred of his deep, continuing personal engagement and experience with some of the most sophisticated and complex spiritual techniques and practices evolved in human history.

To Buddhists around the world, he embodies the epitome of their faith, the highest human aspiration;

for them he is a *bodhisattva,* one who consciously chooses to be born in human form—with its inevitable suffering of old age, sickness, and death—in order to teach and serve humanity.

For more than six million Tibetans, despite China's continuing genocide, the Dalai Lama represents their hope for a future in Tibet where they will be free to revive an old civilization that will synthesize the ancient with the modern, making his vision real. In keeping with Buddhist teachings, he continues his efforts to democratize Tibetans in exile. He has frequently argued that the issue of Tibet is not that of the future of the Dalai Lama, but of the rights and freedoms of all Tibetans inside and outside Tibet. Today, in exile, there is an elected autonomous parliament, a prime minister, and a judiciary. He makes repeated pleas that he be allowed to retire from the temporal leadership of the Tibetan cause; his preeminent global stature and the devotion of his people have meant that he remains its focal point.

To millions around the world, he is simply "His Holiness," familiar for his ever-smiling face and his message of compassion, altruism, and peace.

The Dalai Lama, like all great teachers, embodies what he teaches and practices what he preaches. In his 70s, he follows a regular routine of practices that begins at 4 A.M. every day and continues for several hours. He still receives instructions and initiations from other lamas. For him there has been no single peak, no epiphanic moment, of all-encompassing enlightenment. Although regarded and celebrated as a living Buddha by his followers, he makes no such claims for himself. Like the Buddha, he is an "ordinary" human being like any of us. Through practicing the stages of the path, we can all find happiness and avoid suffering.

His Holiness celebrates diversity, recognizing the uniqueness of each person on our planet—their individual needs, backgrounds, and perspectives. He invites us to learn from his insights and experiences, as we can and must from all traditions, but also advises us to evolve our own journeys of learning and personal growth. The Dalai Lama encourages the most rigorous scrutiny of any teacher or teaching, urging great care before we commit ourselves to any one, and discourages spiritual dilettantes. There are no shortcuts on the path . . . no weekend, weeklong, or short courses to happiness and enlightenment. The journey is the destination, and the time to embark on it is the ever-unfolding present.

The Dalai Lama's eclectic, all-embracing vision has led him to reach out to the wider world, beyond his agendas for the rights of the Tibetan people and his position as one of the great spiritual masters of our time. With a philosophy of inclusiveness, he reaches out to a range of people and groups—to a real dialogue with other faiths; to engaged conversations with scientists, politicians, academics, businesspeople, and activists—so that collectively we can move beyond a syncretic celebration of "unity in diversity" to a deeper understanding of how we can live together in harmony and peace with ourselves, each other, the earth, and the universe. This book invites you to begin this journey with one of the great spiritual and religious masters of all time.

৵৻৶

Chapter One

ON HAPPINESS

One great question underlies our experience, whether we think about it consciously or not: *What is the purpose of life?* I have considered this question and would like to share my thoughts in the hopes that they may be of direct, practical benefit to those who read them.

I believe that the purpose of life is to be happy. From the moment of birth, every human being wants happiness and does not want suffering. Neither social conditioning nor education nor ideology affects this. From the very core of our being, we simply desire contentment. I don't know whether the universe, with its countless galaxies, stars, and planets, has a deeper meaning or not, but—at the very least—it is clear that we humans who live on this earth face the task of making a happy life for ourselves. Therefore, it is important to discover what will bring about the greatest degree of happiness.

For a start, it is possible to divide every kind of happiness and suffering into two main categories: mental and physical. Of the two, it is the mind that exerts the greatest influence on most of us. Unless we are either gravely ill or deprived of basic necessities, our physical condition plays a secondary role in life. If the body is content, we virtually ignore it. The mind, however, registers every event, no matter how small. Hence, we should devote our most serious efforts to bringing about mental peace.

From my own limited experience, I have found that the greatest degree of inner tranquility comes from the development of love and compassion. The more we care for the happiness of others, the greater our own sense of well-being becomes. Cultivating a close, warmhearted feeling for others automatically puts the mind at ease. This helps remove whatever fears or insecurities we may have and gives us the strength to cope with any obstacles we encounter. It is the ultimate source of success in life.

As long as we live in this world, we are bound to encounter problems. If, at such times, we lose hope and become discouraged, we diminish our ability to face difficulties. If, on the other hand, we remember that it is not just ourselves but everyone who has to undergo suffering, this more realistic perspective will increase our determination and capacity to overcome troubles. Indeed, with this attitude, each new obstacle can be seen as yet another valuable opportunity to improve our mind! Thus, we can strive gradually to become more compassionate; that is, we can develop both genuine sympathy for others' suffering and the will to help remove their pain. As a result, our own serenity and inner strength will increase.

Our Need for Love

Ultimately, the reason why love and compassion bring us the greatest happiness is simply that our nature cherishes them above all else. The need for love lies at the very foundation of human existence. It results from the profound interdependence we all share with one another. However capable and skillful an individual may be, left alone he or she will not survive. However vigorous and independent one may feel during the most prosperous periods of life, when one is sick or very young or very old, one must depend on the support of others.

Interdependence, of course, is a fundamental law of nature. Not only higher forms of life, but also many of the smallest insects are social beings who, without any religion, law, or education, survive by mutual cooperation based on an innate recognition of their interconnectedness. The most subtle level of material phenomena is also governed by interdependence. In fact, all phenomena—be they from the oceans, the clouds, or the forests that surround us—arise in dependence upon subtle patterns of energy. Without their proper interaction, they dissolve and decay.

It is because our own human existence is so dependent on the help of others that our need for love lies at the very foundation of our existence. Therefore, we need a genuine sense of responsibility and a sincere concern for the welfare of others.

We have to consider what we human beings really are. We are not like machine-made objects. If we were merely mechanical entities, then machines themselves could alleviate all of our suffering and fulfill our needs. However, since we are not solely material creatures, it is a mistake to place all our hopes for happiness on external development alone. Instead, we should consider our origins and nature to discover who we are and what it is we require.

Leaving aside the complex question of the creation and evolution of our universe, we can at least agree that each of us is the product of our own parents. In general, our conception took place not just in the context of sexual desire, but also from our parents' decision to have a child. Such decisions are founded on responsibility and altruism—the parents' commitment to care for their child until it is able to take care of itself. Thus, from the very moment of our conception, our parents' love is directly in our creation. Moreover, we are completely dependent upon the care of our mothers from the earliest stages of our growth. According to some scientists, a pregnant woman's mental state, be it calm or agitated, has a direct physical effect on her unborn child.

The expression of love is also very important at the time of birth. Since the very first thing we do is suck milk from our mother's breast, we naturally feel close to her, and she must feel love for us in order to feed us properly; if she feels anger or resentment, her milk may not flow freely. Then there is the critical period of brain development from the time of birth up to at least the age of three or four, during which time loving physical contact is the single most important factor for the normal growth of the child. If the child is not held, hugged, cuddled, or loved, its development will be impaired and its brain will not mature properly.

As children grow older and enter school, their need for support must be met by their teachers. If a teacher not only imparts academic education, but also assumes responsibility for preparing students for life, his or her pupils will feel trust and respect, and what has been taught will leave an indelible impression on their minds. On the other hand, that which is taught by a teacher who does not show true concern for his or her students' overall well-being will not be retained for long.

Nowadays, many children grow up in unhappy homes. If they do not receive proper affection, in later life they will rarely love their parents and, not infrequently, will find it hard to love others. This is very sad.

In the end, since a child cannot survive without the care of others, love is its most important nourishment. The happiness of childhood, the allaying of the child's many fears, and the healthy development of its self-confidence all depend directly upon love.

Similarly, if one is sick and being treated at the hospital by a doctor who evinces a warm human feeling, one feels at ease; and the doctor's desire to give the best possible care is itself curative, irrespective of the degree of his or her technical skill. On the other hand, if one's doctor lacks human feeling and displays an unfriendly expression, impatience, or casual disregard, one will feel anxious, even if he or she is the most highly qualified doctor and the disease has been correctly diagnosed and the right medication prescribed. Inevitably, patients' feelings make a difference with respect to the quality and completeness of their recovery.

Even when we engage in ordinary conversation in everyday life, if someone speaks with human feeling, we enjoy listening and respond accordingly; the whole conversation becomes interesting, however unimportant the topic may be. On the other hand, if a person speaks coldly or harshly, we feel uneasy and wish for a quick end to the interaction. From the least to the most important event, the affection and respect of others are vital for our happiness.

Recently I met a group of scientists in America who said that the rate of mental illness in their country was quite high—around 12 percent of the population. It became clear during our discussion that the main cause of depression was not a lack of material necessities, but a deprivation of the affection of others. So, as you can see from everything I have written so far, whether or not we are consciously aware of it, from the day we are born the need for human affection is in our very blood. Even if the affection comes from an animal or someone we would normally consider an enemy, both children and adults will naturally gravitate toward it.

I believe that no one is born free of the need for love. And this demonstrates that, although some modern schools of thought seek to do so, human beings cannot be defined as solely physical. No material object—however beautiful or valuable—can make us feel loved, because our deeper identity and true character lie in the subjective nature of the mind.

Compassion

Some of my friends have told me that while love and compassion are marvelous and good, they are not really very relevant. Our world, they say, is not a place where such beliefs have much influence or power. They claim that anger and hatred are so much a part of human nature that humanity will always be dominated by them. I do not agree.

We humans have existed in our present form for about 100,000 years. I believe that if during this time the human mind had been primarily controlled by anger and hatred, our overall population would have decreased. But today, despite all our wars, we find that the human population is greater than ever. This clearly indicates to me that love and compassion predominate in the world.

And this is why unpleasant events make news; compassionate activities are so much a part of daily life that they are taken for granted and, therefore, largely ignored.

So far I have been mainly discussing the mental benefits of compassion, but it contributes to good physical health as well. According to my personal experience, mental stability and physical well-being are directly related. Without question, anger and agitation make us more susceptible to illness. However, if the mind is tranquil and occupied with positive thoughts, the body will not easily fall prey to disease.

But of course it is also true that we all have an innate self-centeredness that inhibits our love for others. So, since we desire the true happiness that is brought about by only a calm mind, and since such peace of mind is brought about only by a compassionate attitude, how can we develop this? Obviously, it is not enough for us to simply think about how nice compassion is! We need to make a concerted effort to develop it; we must use all the events of our daily life to transform our thoughts and behavior.

First of all, we must be clear about what we mean by compassion. Many forms of compassionate feeling are mixed with desire and attachment. For instance, the love parents feel for their child is often strongly associated with their own emotional needs, so it is not fully compassionate. Again, in marriage, the love between husband and wife—particularly at the beginning, when each partner still may not know the other's deeper character very well—depends more on attachment than genuine love. Our desire can be so strong that the person to whom we are attached appears to be good, when in fact he or she is very negative. In addition, we have a tendency to exaggerate small positive qualities. Thus, when one partner's attitude changes, the other partner is often disappointed and his or her attitude changes, too. This is an indication that love has been motivated more by personal need than by genuine care for the other individual.

True compassion is not just an emotional response, but a firm commitment founded on reason. Therefore, a truly compassionate attitude toward others does not change even if they behave negatively.

Of course, developing this kind of compassion is not at all easy! To start with, let us consider the following facts: Whether people are beautiful and friendly or unattractive and disruptive, ultimately they are human beings, just like oneself. Like oneself, they want happiness and do not want suffering. Furthermore, their right to overcome suffering and be happy is equal to one's own.

Now, when you recognize that all beings are equal in both their desire for happiness and their right to obtain it, you automatically feel empathy and closeness toward them. By accustoming your mind to this sense of universal altruism, you develop a feeling of responsibility for others: the wish to actively help them overcome their problems. Nor is this wish selective; it applies equally to all. As long as they are human beings experiencing pleasure and pain just as you do, there is no logical basis to discriminate between them or to alter your concern for them if they behave negatively.

Let me emphasize that, given patience and time, it is within your power to develop this kind of compassion. Of course, our self-centeredness—our distinctive attachment to the feeling of an independent, self-existent "I"—works fundamentally to inhibit our compassion. Indeed, true compassion can be experienced only when this type of self-grasping is eliminated. But this does not mean that we cannot start and make progress now.

The First Steps Toward Compassion

We should begin by removing the greatest hindrances to compassion: anger and hatred. As we all know, these are extremely powerful emotions, and they can overwhelm our entire mind. Nevertheless, they can be controlled. If, however, they are not, these negative emotions will plague us—with no extra effort on their part!—and impede our quest for the happiness of a loving mind.

So, for a start, it is useful to investigate whether or not anger is of value. Sometimes, when we are discouraged by a difficult situation, anger does seem helpful, appearing to bring with it more energy, confidence, and determination. Here, though, we must examine our mental state carefully. While it is true that anger brings extra energy, if we explore the nature of this energy, we discover that it is blind; we cannot be sure whether its result will be positive or negative. This is because anger eclipses the best part of our brain: its rationality. So, the energy of anger is almost always unreliable. It can cause an immense amount of destructive, unfortunate behavior. Moreover, if anger increases to the extreme, one becomes like a mad person, acting in ways that are as damaging to oneself as they are to others.

It is possible, however, to develop an equally forceful but far more controlled energy with which to handle difficult situations. This controlled energy comes not only from a compassionate attitude, but also from reason and patience. These are the most powerful antidotes to anger. Unfortunately, many people misjudge these qualities as signs of weakness. I believe the opposite to be true: They are the true signs of inner strength. Compassion is by nature gentle, peaceful, and soft, but it is very powerful. It is those who easily lose their patience who are insecure and unstable. Thus, to me, the arousal of anger is a direct sign of weakness.

So, when a problem first arises, try to remain humble, maintain a sincere attitude, and be concerned that the outcome is fair. Of course, others may try to take advantage of you, and if by remaining detached you only encourage unjust aggression, adopt a strong stand. This, however, should be done with compassion, and if it is necessary to express your views and take strong countermeasures, do so without anger or ill intent.

You should realize that even though your opponents appear to be harming you, in the end their destructive activity will damage only themselves. In order to check your own selfish impulse to retaliate, you should recall your desire to practice compassion, and assume responsibility for helping prevent the other person from suffering the consequences of his or her acts. Thus, because the measures you employ have been calmly chosen, they will be more effective, more accurate, and more forceful. Retaliation based on the blind energy of anger seldom hits the target.

Friends and Enemies

I must emphasize again that merely thinking that compassion and reason and patience are good will not be enough to develop them. We must wait for difficulties to arise and then attempt to practice them. And who creates such opportunities? Not our friends, of course, but our enemies. They are the ones who give us the most trouble. So, if we truly wish to learn, we should consider enemies to be our best teacher! For a person who cherishes compassion and love, the practice of tolerance is essential, and for that, an enemy is indispensable. So, we should feel grateful to our enemies, for it is they who can best help us develop a tranquil mind! Also, it is often the case in both personal and public life that with a change in circumstances, enemies become friends.

So, anger and hatred are always harmful, and unless we train our minds and work to reduce their negative force, they will continue to disturb us and disrupt our attempts to develop a calm mind. Anger and hatred are our real enemies. These are the forces we most need to confront and defeat, not the temporary "enemies" who appear intermittently throughout life.

Of course, it is natural and right that we all want friends. I often joke that if you really want to be selfish, you should be very altruistic! You should take good care of others, be concerned for their welfare, help them, serve them, make more friends, make more smiles. The result? When you yourself need help, you find plenty of helpers! If, on the other hand, you neglect the happiness of others, in the long term you will be the loser. And is friendship produced through quarrels and anger, jealousy and intense competitiveness? I do not think so. Only affection brings us genuine close friends.

In today's materialistic society, if you have money and power, you seem to have many friends. But they are not friends of yours; they are the friends of your money and power. When you lose your wealth and influence, you will find it very difficult to track these people down.

The trouble is that when things in the world go well for us, we become confident that we can manage by ourselves, and feel we do not need friends; but as our status and health decline, we quickly realize how wrong we were. That is the moment when we learn who is really helpful and who is completely useless. So, to prepare for that moment, to make genuine friends who will help us when the need arises, we ourselves must cultivate altruism!

Although sometimes people laugh when I say it, I myself always want more friends. I love smiles. Because of this, I have the problem of knowing how to make more friends and how to get more smiles—in particular, genuine smiles. For there are many kinds of smiles, such as sarcastic, artificial, or diplomatic smiles. Many smiles produce no feeling of satisfaction, and sometimes they can even create suspicion or fear, can't they? But a genuine smile really gives us a feeling of freshness, and is, I believe, unique to human beings. If these are the smiles we want, then we ourselves must create the reasons for them to appear.

Compassion and the World

In conclusion, I would like to briefly expand my thoughts beyond the topic of this short piece and make a wider point: Individual happiness can contribute in a profound and effective way to the overall improvement of our entire human community.

Because we all share an identical need for love, it is possible to feel that anybody we meet, in whatever circumstances, is a brother or sister. No matter how new the face or how different the dress and behavior, there is no significant division between us and other people. It is foolish to dwell on external differences, because our basic natures are the same.

Ultimately, humanity is one, and this small planet is our only home. If we are to protect this home of ours, each of us needs to experience a vivid sense of universal altruism. It is only this feeling that can remove the self-centered motives that cause people to deceive and misuse one another. If you have a sincere and open heart, you naturally feel self-worth and confidence, and there is no need to be fearful of others.

I believe that at every level of society—familial, tribal, national, and international—the key to a happier and more successful world is the growth of compassion. We do not need to become religious, nor do we need to believe in an ideology. All that is necessary is for each of us to develop our good human qualities.

I try to treat whomever I meet as an old friend. This gives me a genuine feeling of happiness. It is the practice of compassion.

᠋᛫᠋᛫᠋᛫

Chapter Two

WHAT IS BUDDHISM?

To practice Buddhism is to wage a struggle between the negative and positive forces in your mind. The meditator seeks to undermine the negative, and develop and increase the positive.

There are no physical markers by which to measure progress in the struggle between the positive and negative forces in consciousness. Changes begin when you first identify and recognize your delusions, such as anger and jealousy. One then needs to know the antidotes to delusion, and that knowledge is gained by listening to the teachings. There is no simple way to remove delusions. They cannot be extracted surgically. They have to be recognized, and then, through the practice of these teachings, they can be gradually reduced and then completely eliminated.

These teachings offer the means to free oneself from delusion—a path that eventually leads to freedom from all suffering and to the bliss of enlightenment. The more one comes to understand the *Dharma,* or Buddhist teachings, the weaker will be the grip of pride, hatred, greed, and other negative emotions that cause so much suffering. Applying this understanding to daily life over a period of months and years will gradually transform the mind because, despite the fact that it often seems otherwise, the mind is subject to change. If you can compare your state of mind now to your state of mind after you have read this book, you may notice some improvement. If so, these teachings will have served their purpose.

The word *dharma* in Sanskrit means "that which holds." All existents are dharmas, phenomena, in the sense that they hold or bear their own entity or character. Also, a religion is a dharma in the sense that it holds persons back or protects them from disasters. Here the term *Dharma* refers to the latter definition. In rough terms, any elevated action of body, speech, or mind is regarded as a dharma because through such an action, one is protected or held back from all sorts of disasters. The practice of such actions is the practice of Dharma.

The Buddha

Buddha Shakyamuni was born more than 2,500 years ago in India. He took birth as a prince. Even as a child he was mature in terms of both his knowledge and his compassion. He saw that by nature we all want happiness and do not want suffering.

Suffering is not something that always comes from the outside. It does not only involve problems like famine and drought. If this were the case, we could protect ourselves from suffering, for example, by storing food. But sufferings such as sickness, aging, and death are problems related to the very nature of our existence, and we cannot overcome them by changing external conditions. What is more, we have within us this untamed mind, susceptible to all kinds of problems. It is afflicted with negative thoughts like doubt and anger. As long as our minds are beset by this host of negative thoughts, even if we have soft, comfortable clothes and delicious food to eat, they will not solve our problems.

Motivated by compassion for all sentient beings, Buddha Shakyamuni observed all these problems, and he reflected on the nature of his own existence. He found that all human beings undergo suffering, and he saw that we experience this unhappiness because of our undisciplined state of mind. He saw that our minds are so wild that often we cannot even sleep at night. Faced with these dilemmas, he was wise enough to ask whether there is a method to overcome these problems.

He decided that living the life of a prince in a palace was not the way to eliminate suffering. If anything, it was a hindrance. So he gave up all the comforts of the palace, including the companionship of his wife and son, and embarked on the homeless life. In the course of his search, he consulted many teachers and listened to their instructions. He found that their teachings were of some use, but they did not provide an ultimate solution to the problem of how to eliminate suffering.

He undertook six years of strict asceticism. By giving up all that he had enjoyed as a prince and engaging in strict ascetic practice, he was able to strengthen his meditative understanding. Seated beneath the bodhi tree (sacred fig tree), he overcame the obstructive forces and attained enlightenment.

Subsequently, he began to teach, to turn the wheel of doctrine, based on his own experience and realization.

When we talk about the Buddha, we are not talking about someone who was a Buddha from the beginning. He began just like us. He was an ordinary sentient being who saw the same suffering we do: birth, old age, sickness, and death. He had various thoughts and feelings—happy feelings and feelings of pain—just as we do. But as a result of his strong and integrated spiritual practice, he was able to achieve the various levels of the spiritual path culminating in enlightenment.

Sometimes when I reflect on the life of Buddha Shakyamuni, I have a sense of unease. Although Buddha Shakyamuni's teaching can be interpreted on various levels, it is evident from historical accounts that Buddha Shakyamuni underwent six years of hard practice. This shows that the mind cannot be transformed merely by sleeping and relaxing and enjoying all of life's comforts. It shows us that only through working hard and undergoing hardship over a long period of time will we be able to attain enlightenment.

It is not easy to attain all the spiritual levels and realizations within a short time without making any effort. Even the Buddha, the proponent of the teaching we are following, had to undergo such hardship. How, then, can we expect to attain spiritual heights and become enlightened merely by performing certain so-called practices and having a relaxing time? If we read the stories of the great spiritual teachers of the past, we find that they have attained spiritual realization through a great deal of meditation, solitude, and practice. They did not take any shortcuts.

The root of suffering is ignorance, which here means the misconception of self. All the myriad sufferings we encounter arise because of this misconception, this wrong understanding. Therefore, when it is said that the Buddha discarded all wrong views out of compassion, it means that he had the compassion to work for the benefit of all sentient beings. In order to benefit sentient beings, he gave various levels of teachings that are free from wrong views and negative thoughts. Therefore, those who follow these teachings, by understanding the right view and putting it into practice, will be able to eliminate suffering. We pay homage to Buddha Shakyamuni because he gave such sublime teachings.

The principal motive impelling the Buddha to achieve all his great qualities of body, speech, and mind was compassion. The essence of our practice, too, should be the wish to help others. Such an altru-istic wish is naturally present within our hearts in the acknowledgment that others are just like us in wishing to be happy and avoiding suffering. It is like a seed, which we can protect and help to grow through practice. All the teachings of the Buddha essentially try to develop this kind heart and altruis-tic mind.

The Buddha's path is founded on compassion, the wish that others be free from suffering. This leads us to the understanding that the welfare of others is ultimately more important than our own, for without others, we would have no spiritual practice, no oppor-tunity for enlightenment. I do not claim to have great knowledge or high realization, but remembering the kindness of my teachers, who gave these instructions to me, and with concern for the welfare of all beings, I offer these teachings to you.

Dharma in Tibet

This precious human life as a free and fortu-nate human being can be obtained just once. Even though we have had countless lives in the past, we have never yet been able to put such a precious human life to proper use. Today, we are fortunate to have found a life in which our mental and physical faculties are intact, and we have some interest in practicing the Dharma. Such a life is unique. Similarly, the Dharma we have access to is unique. It first derived from the Buddha in India, and it was passed down by subsequent great Indian masters.

Gradually it came to flourish in Tibet, and that tradition of Buddhist practice is still very much alive. In Tibet, the Land of Snows, we have maintained the complete range of practice of the teachings of the Buddha. Therefore, at this time it is extremely important that we make a concerted effort to use it to fulfill the best purposes of ourselves and all other sentient beings.

Buddhism did not come to Tibet until the 8th century, and in the 9th century its practice was outlawed by King Lang-dar-ma. He closed the monasteries, which had been the primary centers for teachings, as the Chinese have done today. Lang-dar-ma's destruction of Buddhism was extensive, but it was still possible to practice in remote regions, and the tradition was preserved.

In the 11th century, confusion arose over the existence of two approaches to the practice of the teachings: There was *sutra*, or the path of study and practice by which it takes many lifetimes to achieve enlightenment; and *tantra,* the secret practices by which enlightenment can be achieved even in one lifetime. In the 11th century, an Indian monk named Atisha became famous for his ability to explain the Buddha's teachings and defend them in debates with non-Buddhist philosophers. He was able to bring together all the diverse Buddhist philosophical positions that had developed over the centuries, as well as the lay and monastic systems of practice. He was regarded as a nonpartisan and authoritative master by all the philosophical schools.

Within Tibetan Buddhism there are four schools: Nyingma, Sakya, Geluk, and Kagyu. It is a great mistake to claim that one of these schools is superior to the others. They all follow the same master, the Buddha Shakyamuni; they have all combined the systems of sutra and tantra. I try to cultivate faith and admiration for all four schools. I do it not just as a diplomatic gesture, but out of strong conviction. It also befits my position as the Dalai Lama to know enough about the teachings of all four schools to be able to offer advice to those who come to me. Otherwise, I am like a mother with no arms watching a child drown.

There was a meditator from the Nyingma school who once came and asked me about a certain practice that I did not know well. I was able to send him to a great master who could answer his question, but I felt depressed that he had come sincerely seeking a teaching from me and I could not fulfill his wish. It is one thing if another's wish is beyond one's ability to fulfill, but so long as it is within one's own ability, it is very important to meet the spiritual needs of as many sentient beings as possible. We must study all the aspects of the teachings and develop admiration for them.

Nor should we consider Tibetan Buddhism to be superior to other forms of Buddhism. In Thailand, Burma, and Sri Lanka, the monks have a true commitment to the practice of monastic discipline; and unlike Tibetan monks, they still maintain the custom of begging for meals, which was practiced 2,500 years ago by the Buddha and his disciples. In Thailand I joined a group of monks on their rounds. It was a hot, sunny day; and because the tradition is to go without shoes, my feet really burned. It was inspiring to see the practice of the Thai monks.

These days, many people see only negativity in the practice of a spiritual tradition or religion. They see only how religious institutions exploit the masses and take away their possessions. However, the faults they see are not faults of the traditions themselves, but of the persons who claim to be followers of such traditions, like the members of monasteries or churches who use spiritual excuses for bettering themselves at the expense of other adherents. If spiritual practitioners themselves are careless, it reflects upon everyone involved in that practice. Attempts to correct institutionalized faults are often misconstrued as an attack on the tradition as a whole.

Many people conclude that religion is harmful and cannot help them. They reject any form of faith. Others are totally indifferent to spiritual practice and are satisfied with their worldly way of life. They have physical and material comforts and are neither for nor against religion. Yet all are equal in that they have the instinctive wish to gain happiness and avoid suffering.

In Buddhist practice, instead of avoiding these sufferings, we deliberately visualize them—the sufferings of birth, the sufferings of aging, the sufferings of fluctuations in status, the sufferings of uncertainty within this lifetime, and the sufferings of death. We deliberately try to think of them so that when we actually do face them, we are prepared. When we meet with death, we will realize that our time has come. That does not mean that we would not protect our bodies. When we are sick, we take medicines and try to avert death. But if death is unavoidable, then the Buddhist will be prepared.

Let us set aside for the moment the question of life after death, liberation, or the omniscient state. Even within this lifetime, thinking about the Dharma and belief in the Dharma have practical benefits. In Tibet, although the Chinese have meted out such systematic destruction and torture, the people still have not lost their hope and their determination. I think it is because of the Buddhist tradition.

Although the destruction of Buddhism has not gone on for as long under Chinese rule as it did under Lang-dar-ma in the 9th century, the extent of destruction is far greater. When Lang-dar-ma had destroyed the Dharma, it was Atisha who came to Tibet and restored the entire practice of Buddhism. Now, whether we are capable or not, the responsibility has fallen on all of us to restore that which has been systematically destroyed by the Chinese. Buddhism is a treasure meant for the entire world. To teach and to listen to this teaching is a contribution to the wealth of humanity. There might be many points that you are not able to practice immediately, but keep them in your heart so that you will be able to practice them next year or after five or ten years— as long as the teachings are not forgotten.

Although we exiled Tibetans are struck by the tragedy of losing our country, we remain generally free from obstacles in the practice of the Dharma. In whatever country we reside in, we have access to the Buddha's teachings through exiled teachers, and we know how to create conditions conducive to meditation. Tibetans have been doing this at least since the 8th century. Those who remained in Tibet after the Chinese invasion in the 1950s have had to undergo great physical and mental suffering. Monasteries were emptied, great teachers were imprisoned, and the practice of Buddhism became punishable by imprisonment or even death.

We must use all opportunities to practice the truth, to improve ourselves, instead of waiting for a time when we think we will be less busy. The activities of this world are like ripples in a pond: When one disappears, another emerges; there is no end to them. Worldly activities do not stop until the time of death; we should try to search for a time within our own daily lives to practice the Dharma. At this juncture —when we have obtained the precious human form and have met with the Dharma and have some faith in it—if we are not able to put the Dharma into practice, it will be difficult for us to undertake its practice in future lifetimes, when we will not have such conditions. Now that we have met with such a profound system, in which the entire method for the achievement of the enlightened state is accessible, it would be very sad if we did not try to make the Dharma have some impact on our lives.

❦❦❦

Chapter Three

ESSENTIAL
BUDDHIST TEACHINGS

The Four Noble Truths

The Buddha arose from meditation 2,500 years ago after attaining enlightenment. The subject of his first teaching was the Four Noble Truths.

The First Noble Truth is the truth of suffering, the fact that our happiness is constantly passing away. Everything we have is subject to impermanence. Nothing within what we commonly think of as real is permanent. Ignorance, attachment, and anger are the causes of our relentless suffering. Thus, the Second Noble Truth is to understand this cause of suffering. When you eliminate the root of suffering (the delusions), you achieve a state of cessation of suffering —the Third Noble Truth, or *nirvana*. The Fourth Noble Truth is that there exists a path leading to the cessation of suffering. In order to achieve that state within your own mind, you must follow a path.

In order to understand these four truths, it is necessary to recognize that they are rooted in two other truths—namely, relative and absolute truth. At the level of relative truth, this and that, I and other . . . each seems to have an independent existence of its own. But from the viewpoint of absolute truth, every object and every being is found to exist only in dependence on all other existing entities.

With this perception comes the understanding of the ultimate mode of existence—namely, the complete absence of independent or inherent isolated existence of anything whatsoever. This ultimate nature of phenomena is called emptiness, and these two differing concepts of it are known as the conventional and the ultimate modes of phenomena. Understanding these two truths of the true nature of phenomena, one sees that they arise in dependence upon conditions and that they completely lack an independent existence of their own. When certain conditions come together, then phenomena arise; if the cooperative conditions do not come together, or if they should cease, then these phenomena do not exist. So this, then, is the process by which phenomena arise and pass away.

In explaining the Four Noble Truths, I will do so not in the context of one individual, but rather in the context of the whole of mankind or of this world community, this human society. So now, first of all comes the first truth, the truth of suffering. There is a wide variety of suffering, but now the most frightening, the most serious, is that of war. The situation of the world is one in which there is danger not only to the life of each individual, but rather to the lives of the population of this entire planet.

Next, upon searching for the source of the suffering, one finds that this source is in the mind: specifically, in mental factors and such mental distortions as attachment and anger, as well as an evil related to anger—namely, jealousy. Anger, hatred, and so on are the actual source of suffering. Certainly there are also external weapons, but these weapons themselves are not the source of the problem because they need to be employed by human beings; they cannot work by themselves, and in order for human beings to employ them, there have to be motivations. These motivations are mainly hatred and attachment, especially hatred.

This is a vicious state of mind. If we have contentment, happiness, or tranquility, we have inner peace. If we do not have inner or mental peace, how can we have external peace? It will not do to drop atom bombs on people; in seeking the establishment of peace, one has to turn to the mind. To destroy mental defects, external weapons are of no use at all. The only way is to endeavor to control one's own mind.

Coming now to the truth of the cessation of suffering: It is clear that the cessation of mental distortions such as anger and jealousy, although they can ultimately be eradicated, is something to look for in the future. What can be done now is to try to foresee the future. A clear understanding of what seems likely to be our future would surely reduce such mental defects as anger. To reduce anger effectively requires that we avoid the conditions that lead to anger, such as pride and jealousy. We must try to abandon these and, on the other hand, accustom ourselves to states of mind that are incongruous with jealousy and pride. That it is possible to lessen such mental distortions is something that can be verified.

The truth of the path to the cessation of suffering has as its very root . . . compassion. This involves developing a mind of kindness and kindheartedness—that is to say, developing motivation toward the service and benefit of others. This is the very essence of the path to the cessation of suffering. To cultivate compassion, it is necessary to minimize the effects of such divisions among humanity as race, culture, appearance, and varying philosophical traditions. Putting aside these classifications, one becomes very much aware of the fact that human beings are human beings and have this great factor in common, whether we are Easterners or Westerners, believers or nonbelievers: All of us are human beings—that is to say, beings of the same kind. From this recognition will come a true sense of brotherhood, a love for one another, more concern for others, less selfishness. These things are essential. This kind of effort is indeed difficult, but it is also worthwhile.

The Blessed One said, "These are true sufferings, these are true sources, these are true cessations, these are true paths. Sufferings are to be known, their sources are to be abandoned, their cessations are to be actualized, the paths are to be cultivated. Sufferings are to be known; then, there will be no more sufferings to be known. The sources of sufferings are to be abandoned; then, there will be no more sources to be abandoned. The cessations of suffering are to be actualized; then, there will be no more cessations to be actualized. The paths are to be cultivated; then, there will be no more paths to be cultivated." These are the Four Noble Truths in terms of their entities, requisite actions, and actions together with their effects.

The Eightfold Path

The path is the essence of the way to live a Buddhist life. Following it crushes the seeds of innate delusions. The noble path of definite release consists of *right view, right thought, right speech, right conduct, right livelihood, right effort, right mindfulness,* and *right meditative stabilization.* Their nature and functions are as follows:

- **Right view** is to discern the view through analytical means in the post-meditational period, thinking, *This is what I have realized during meditative equipoise as to the reality of the Four Noble Truths.*

- **Right thought** is to examine how the profound meaning already understood through correct reasons and signs complies with the meaning of the sutras so that its significance may be understood and explained to others.

- **Right speech** is to show others—by means of teaching, debate, and writing—the nature of reality free from elaboration as it is represented conventionally by mere words, and to lead them to the conviction that it is the perfect view. This is pure speech, free from deceit, etc.

- **Right conduct** is pure behavior convincing others that all our activities conform with the doctrine and are harmonious with pure ethics.

- **Right livelihood** is to convince others that our livelihood is proper, not mixed with the evil fruits of wrong livelihood, and free from wheedling behavior, flattering speech, and so forth.

- **Right effort** is to meditate repeatedly on the meaning of reality that has already been seen, which is thereby an antidote to the delusions to be abandoned on the path of meditation.

- **Right mindfulness** is to retain the object of calm abiding and insight meditation without forgetting it, which acts as an antidote to the secondary delusion forgetfulness.

- **Right meditative stabilization** is to establish meditative stabilization free from the faults of stabilization laxity and excitement, which acts as an antidote to hindrances and leads to the progressive attainment of the qualities of the path.

Basic Ethics

Even though the training in ethics takes many forms, abandoning the ten nonvirtues forms their basis. Of the ten nonvirtues, three pertain to bodily actions, four to verbal actions, and three to mental actions.

The three physical nonvirtues are:

- **Taking the life of a living being:** ranging from killing an insect to killing a human

- **Stealing:** taking away another's property without his consent, regardless of its value, whether the deed is done by oneself or through another

- **Sexual misconduct:** committing adultery

The four verbal nonvirtues are:

- **Lying:** deceiving others through spoken words or physical gestures

- **Divisiveness:** creating dissension by causing those in agreement to disagree or by causing those in disagreement to disagree even further

- **Harshness:** abusing others

- **Senselessness:** talking about foolish things motivated by desire and so forth

The three mental nonvirtues are:

- **Covetousness:** thinking, *May this become mine,* desiring something that belongs to another

- **Harmful intent:** wishing to injure others, be it great or small injury

- **Wrong view:** viewing some existent thing—such as rebirth, cause and effect, or the Three Jewels (the Buddha, his Doctrine, and the Spiritual Community)—as nonexistent

Choosing a Teacher

It is common knowledge that to achieve the desired results, it is essential to gather the conducive factors and eliminate obstacles. We plan in advance, whether we are working on developments in science and technology or economics or any other area.

When we follow the steps we have laid out, we are almost certain to achieve the result we are aiming for. Since the purpose of Dharma practice is ultimately to achieve enlightenment, we must be very careful how we plan and implement our course of action. Therefore, it is very important to find a suitable and qualified spiritual teacher.

The person you take as a spiritual master should be someone qualified. He or she should at least be gentle and have tamed his or her own mind, because the very purpose of adopting someone as your spiritual master is to tame the mind. This means that the spiritual master should be someone who has achieved realizations through constant practice.

Since the spiritual master plays a crucial role in our quest for realization, the Buddha has defined his or her qualifications at great length. To summarize a spiritual master's essential qualities, the person should be true to his or her practice and rich in knowledge of the Dharma. Therefore, it is essential that we examine a potential spiritual master before establishing a master-disciple relationship with that person. It is absolutely fine to listen to his or her teachings, for such contact will provide us with first-hand experience of the person's teaching ability. To evaluate the person's personal practice, we can examine his or her lifestyle. We can also learn about the person from people who already know him or her. It is also useful to get to know the person in other contexts.

So, when you feel confident, you should then seek to adopt that person as your spiritual master. Once you have accepted someone as your spiritual master, it is essential to cultivate a proper sense of faith and respect and abide by his or her spiritual instructions. It is important to be clear that faith and respect do not imply *blind* faith. On the contrary, there should be a more informed approach. In the sutras, the Buddha explains that a disciple should abide by the spiritual master's virtuous instructions but disregard his or her unwholesome commands. The texts on discipline follow a similar line, stating that you should not accept anything a teacher suggests that does not accord with the Dharma.

The main criterion for deciding whether a teacher's instruction is acceptable or not is to see whether it conforms to fundamental Buddhist principles. When it does, we should respectfully obey. Such a teaching is sure to produce positive results. When a teacher's advice contradicts Buddhist principles, we should hesitate and seek clarification. For instance, if an ordained person were told to drink alcohol, it would contradict the vows of ordination. So, unless the teacher gave a special reason for doing so, it would be wiser to ignore the teacher's command.

In short, the spiritual master should be proficient in the three trainings in ethics, meditation, and wisdom. This, in turn, requires an understanding of the three sets of discourses, which implies that he or she should have knowledge of the scriptures. The spiritual master should be someone who can answer your questions directly and clarify your doubts, and whose outward appearance and behavior indicates or complies with inner realization. There is a saying that the stripes of the tiger are visible, but those of human beings are not; still, we can infer what other people are like from the way they appear to us.

After you have found and developed faith in a spiritual master, it is important to avoid a breakdown in your relationship. So how should you relate to such a being?

We can think in this way: *Since the Buddhas are actively engaged in working for the welfare of sentient beings, and we are among those seeking liberation, there should be a medium by which we can receive their inspiration and blessing.* This is the role of the spiritual master, for it is the spiritual master who brings about a transformation within our minds.

༺☙༻

Chapter Four

THE LAW OF KARMA

Imagine a wide ocean with a golden yoke adrift upon it. In the depths of the ocean swims a single blind turtle, who surfaces for air once every hundred years. How rare would it be for the turtle to surface with its head through the hole in the yoke? The Buddha said that attaining a precious human rebirth is rarer than that.

It is said that even the gods envy our human existence because it is the best form of existence for the practice of the Dharma. There are something like five billion people in this world, and all of them are human beings—their hands, brains, limbs, and bodies are quite the same. But if we examine whether all humans have the opportunity for practice, then we will find differences. We are free from adverse circumstances that prevent the practice of the Dharma—adverse circumstances such as rebirth with wrong views; rebirth as an animal, ghost, or hell being . . . or as a god addicted to pleasure or as a human who has difficulty hearing the teachings; or being born into a place where there is no Buddhist teaching available. Other adverse circumstances would be to be born in a barbarous land where thoughts of survival consume all one's resources, or at a time when no Buddha has appeared.

On the positive side, we are endowed with many things that make our practice possible. For example, we have been born as humans able to respond to the teachings in lands where the teachings are available. We have not committed any heinous crimes and have a degree of faith in the Buddhist teachings. Although we have not taken rebirth in the world when the Buddha was alive, we have met with spiritual masters who can trace the lineage of the teachings they have received all the way back to the Buddha. The Dharma remains stable and flourishing because there are practitioners following these teachings. We also live in a time when there are kind benefactors who provide monks and nuns with necessities for practice, such as food, clothing, and shelter.

It is said that the doctrine of Buddha Shakya-muni will remain for 5,000 years. If we take rebirth as a human after that, we will not benefit from it. But we have taken rebirth in this world during an eon of illumination, when the Buddha's doctrine still remains. In order to want to transform the mind, you must be persuaded to take full advantage of your life as a human being.

Up to this point, we have been living our lives, we have been eating, we have found shelter, and we have been wearing clothes. If we were to continue in this same manner, simply eating for the sake of living, what meaning does that give our lives? We have all obtained a precious human form, but in itself it is nothing to be proud of. There are an infinite number of other forms of life on the planet, but none are engaged in the kind of destruction in which humans indulge. Human beings endanger all living things on the planet.

If we let compassion and an altruistic attitude guide our lives, we will be able to achieve great things—something that other forms of life are not able to do. If we are able to use this precious human form in a positive manner, it will have value in the long term. Our human existence will then become truly precious. If, however, we use our human potential—the ability of the brain—in negative ways to torture people, exploit others, and cause destruction, then our human existence will be a danger to ourselves in the future, as well as to others right now. Human existence, if used destructively, has the potential to annihilate everything we know. Or, it can be the source for becoming a Buddha.

Cause and Effect

We have been propelled into the cycle of suffering by our delusions and the actions they provoke, which are known as *karma*. Because of the cause-and-effect relationship between our actions and our experience, we spend our lives enduring all sorts of ups and downs, in trouble and confusion. To be totally free from the weight of past deeds and from the thralldom of desire, hatred, and ignorance is called liberation, or *nirvana*. When we are able to eliminate delusions and karma by realizing the natural purity of the mind, total peace follows, and we gain complete freedom from the cycle of suffering.

If we can do good deeds, such as saving the lives of animals under threat of death, we can accumulate the conditions necessary for gaining rebirth as a human being. If we undertake serious practice of the Dharma, we will be able to continue our spiritual progress in our lives to come. But this life is precious and unpredictable, and it is important to engage in practice while we have the opportunity. We never know how long that opportunity will last.

What we do now, according to the law of karma—the principle of cause and effect—has consequences for the future. Our future is determined by our present state of mind, but our present state of mind is overrun by delusions. We should aspire to achieve enlightenment. If that is not possible, we should seek to gain freedom from rebirth. If that is not possible, we should at least plant the seeds for a favorable rebirth in the next life, without falling into lower realms of existence. At this auspicious juncture, when we are free of obstacles to hearing and practicing the Dharma, we must not let this rare opportunity pass.

Karma can be understood as cause and effect in much the same way that a physicist understands that for every action there is an equal and opposite reaction. As with physics, what form that reaction will take is not always predictable, but sometimes we can predict the reaction and we can do something to mitigate the outcome.

Science is working on ways to clean up the environment now that it has been polluted, and many more scientists are attempting to prevent further pollution. In the same way, our future lives are determined by our present actions, as well as those of our immediate past and past lives. The practice of the Dharma is meant to mitigate the outcome of our karmic actions and prevent any further pollution by negative thoughts and actions. Those negative thoughts and actions will otherwise land us in a rebirth of tremendous suffering. Sooner or later we are going to die, so sooner or later we will have to take rebirth again. The realms of existence where we can take rebirth are confined to two: the favorable and the unfavorable. When we take rebirth depends on karma.

Consciousness and Rebirth

Karma is created by an agent, a person, a living being. Living beings are nothing other than the self, imputed on the basis of the continuity of consciousness. The nature of consciousness is luminosity and clarity. It is an agent of knowing that is preceded by an earlier moment of consciousness that is its cause.

If we come to understand that the continuity of consciousness cannot be exhausted within one lifetime, we will find that there is logical support for the possibility of life after death. If we are not convinced of the continuity of consciousness, at least we know that there is no evidence that can disprove the theory of life after death. We cannot prove it, but we cannot disprove it.

There are many cases of people remembering their past lives vividly. It is not a phenomenon confined to Buddhists. There are people with such memories whose parents do not believe in life after death or past lives. I know of three cases of children who have been able to remember their past lives vividly. In one case the recollection of the past life was so vivid that even though the parents previously did not believe in life after death, as a result of the clarity of their child's recollections, they are now convinced. The child not only recollected clearly having lived in a nearby village that she recognized, but was able to identify her previous parents, whom she had no other occasion to know.

If there is no life after death—there is no past life—then we will have to find another explanation for these recollections. There are also many cases of parents who have two children brought up in the same way, in the same society, with the same background, yet one is more successful than the other. We find that such differences come about as a result of differences in our past karmic actions.

Death is nothing other than the separation of consciousness from the physical body. If you do not accept this phenomenon called consciousness, then I think it would also be very difficult to explain exactly what life is. When consciousness is connected to the body and their relationship continues, we call it life; and when consciousness terminates its relationship with a particular body, we call it death. Although our bodies are an aggregation of chemical or physical components, a kind of subtle agent of pure luminosity constitutes the life of living beings. Since it is not physical, we cannot measure it, but that does not mean that it does not exist. We have spent so much time, energy, and research in the exploration of the external world, but now if we change that approach and direct all this exploration, research, and energy inward and begin to analyze, I really think we have the ability to realize the nature of consciousness—this clarity, this luminosity—within ourselves.

According to the Buddhist explanation, consciousness is said to be non-obstructive and non-physical, and it is from the actions of this consciousness that all emotions, all delusions, and all human faults arise. However, it is also because of the inherent nature of this consciousness that one can eliminate all these faults and delusions and bring about lasting peace and happiness. Since consciousness is the basis for existence and enlightenment, there are extensive writings on the topic.

We know from our own experience that consciousness or mind is subject to change, which implies that it is dependent upon causes and conditions that change, transform, and influence it: the conditions and circumstances of our lives. Consciousness must have a substantial cause similar to the nature of consciousness itself in order for it to arise. Without a prior moment of consciousness there cannot be any consciousness. It does not arise out of nothing, and it cannot turn into nothing. Matter cannot change into consciousness. Therefore, we should be able to trace the causal sequence of moments of consciousness back in time.

The Buddhist scriptures speak of hundreds of billions of world systems—infinite numbers of world systems—and consciousness existing since beginningless time. I believe that other worlds exist. Modern cosmology also says that there are many different types of world systems. Although life has not been scientifically observed on other planets, it would be illogical to conclude that life is possible only on this planet, which is dependent upon this solar system, and not on other types of planets. Buddhist scriptures mention the presence of life in other world systems, as well as different types of solar systems and an infinite number of universes.

Now if the scientists are asked how the universe came about, they have a lot of answers to give. But if they are asked why this evolution took place, then they have no answers. They generally do not explain it as God's creation, because they are objective observers who tend only to believe in the material universe. Some say that it happened just by chance. Now that position itself is illogical because if anything exists by chance, then it is tantamount to saying that things do not have any causes. But we see from our everyday lives that everything has a cause: Clouds cause rain; the wind blows seeds around so that new plants grow. Nothing exists without any reason.

If evolution has a cause, then there are two possible explanations: You can accept that the universe was created by God, in which case there will be a lot of contradictions, such as the necessity that suffering and evil must also have been created by God; the other option is to explain that there are infinite numbers of sentient beings whose karmic potentials collectively created this entire universe as an environment for them. The universe we inhabit is created by our own desires and actions. This is why we are here. This, at least, is logical.

At the time of death, we are blown about by the force of our own karmic actions. The result of negative karmic actions is rebirth in the lower realms. In order to discourage ourselves from negative actions, we should try to imagine whether we would be able to bear the suffering of the lower realms. Having seen that happiness is a consequence of positive actions, we will take great pleasure in accumulating virtue.

Equating your own experience with that of others, you will be able to develop strong compassion, for you will understand that their sufferings are no different from your own, and they also wish to achieve liberation.

It is important to meditate upon the suffering of the animal and hell realms. If we do not make spiritual progress, our negative actions will lead us there. And if we feel we cannot bear the suffering of burning or cold or unquenchable thirst, then our motivation to practice will increase immeasurably. At the present time, this human existence affords us the opportunity and conditions to rescue ourselves.

The Consequences of Karma

The consequences of karma are definite: Negative actions always bring about suffering, and positive actions always bring happiness. If you do good, you will have happiness; if you do bad, you yourself suffer. Our karmic actions follow us through multiple lifetimes, which explains why some people who indulge constantly in negativity are still successful at the worldly level or why others who are committed to spiritual practice face myriad difficulties. Karmic actions have been committed in infinite numbers of lives, so there is infinite potential for an infinite number of outcomes.

The potential of karma always increases over time. Small seeds have the potential to produce massive fruits. That is also true of the inner cause and effect: Even a small action can bring about a massive consequence, whether positive or negative. For example, a small boy once offered the Buddha a handful of sand, vividly imagining it to be gold. In a further life, the boy was reborn as the great Buddhist emperor Ashoka. From the slightest positive action can come the greatest consequence of happiness, and in the same way, the smallest negative action can bring about very intense suffering. The potential of karma to increase within our mindstreams is far greater than the potential of mere physical causes, such as an apple seed. Just as drops of water can fill a large vessel, in the same way, the smallest actions, when continuously committed, can fill the minds of sentient beings.

Within the human community we see a lot of differences. Some people are always successful in their lives; some are always unsuccessful. Some are happy; some have a good presence and calmness of mind. Some people always seem to face great misfortune, against our expectations. Some people whom you would expect to have misfortune do not. All of this testifies to the fact that not everything is within our hands. Sometimes when we try to start an endeavor, we accumulate all the necessary conditions that are required for its success, but still something is missing. We say that someone is lucky and someone is unlucky, but this alone is not enough; luck must have a reason, a cause.

According to the Buddhist explanation, it is the consequence of your actions committed either in the past life or in the earlier part of this life. When the potential has ripened, then even if you are facing adverse circumstances, the endeavor proves successful. But in some cases, even if you have gathered all the necessary conditions, you fail.

We Tibetans have become refugees and have undergone a lot of suffering, but still we are relatively fortunate and successful. In Tibet, the Chinese have tried to make the entire population equal by creating communes and limiting private property. But still, in the communes, some gardens grow more vegetables than others, and some cows give more milk. This shows that there is a great difference between the merits of individuals. If someone's virtuous actions ripen, even though the authorities confiscate his or her wealth, this person will still prove successful because of the force of his or her merit, because of the force of that karma.

If you accumulate virtuous actions properly—such as avoiding killing, freeing animals, and cultivating patience toward others—it will be beneficial in the future and in the lives to come; whereas if you indulge in negative actions continuously, you definitely will face the consequences in the future. If you do not believe in the principle of karma, then you can do as you like.

Positive and negative actions are determined by one's own motivation. If the motivation is good, all actions become positive; if the motivation is wrong, all actions become negative. The karmic actions are of many different types: Some are totally virtuous, some are totally nonvirtuous, some are mixed. If the motivation is right, although the action itself might appear quite violent, it will bring about happiness. If, however, the motivation is wrong and devious, then even though the action might seem beneficial and positive, in reality it will be a negative action. It all depends upon the mind: If your mind is tamed and trained, all actions become positive; whereas if your mind is not tamed and it is influenced constantly by desire and hatred, although actions might appear to be positive, in reality you will accumulate negative karma.

If more people believed in the law of karma, we would likely never have to have a police force or a penal system. But if individuals lack this internal faith in karmic actions, even though externally people might apply all sorts of techniques to execute the law, they will not be able to bring about a peaceful society. In this modern world, sophisticated equipment is used for surveillance and for detecting lawbreakers. But the more fascinating and sophisticated these machines are, the more sophisticated and determined criminals become. If this human society is to change for the better, then enforcing a law externally alone will not be enough: We need some kind of internal deterrent.

The Enemy Within

Delusion is the chief cause of rebirth in *samsara,* or the cyclic existence. Without delusions karmic actions would not have the power to produce rebirth; they would be like seeds that have been burned. It is very important to seek the antidotes to the delusions, and that in turn depends upon whether or not you have identified the delusions properly. Therefore, we should be very clear about the general and individual characteristics of the delusions. As the First Dalai Lama said, tame the one enemy within, which is delusion. External enemies might seem very harmful, but in future lives they could turn into our friends. Even now they provide us with the opportunity to practice patience and compassion, because we are all basically the same: We all want happiness and do not want suffering. But the inner enemy, the enemy of delusion, has no positive qualities: It is only to be fought and destroyed. We thus have to identify the enemy properly and see how it operates. Any mental state that destroys calmness of mind and brings about mental misery—which upsets, afflicts, and torments the mind—is said to be a delusion.

Let us identify some of the chief delusions:

— First, there is **attachment,** which is the strong desire for beautiful persons, beautiful things, or pleasurable experiences. Attachment is very difficult to get rid of; it is as if your mind has become fixed to the object.

— Another delusion is **anger.** When people become angry, we can immediately see that they lose their composure; their faces become red and wrinkled, and even their eyes become red. The object of anger, whether animate or inanimate, is found to be undesirable and repulsive. Anger is an untamed state of mind, very rough and uneven.

— Another delusion, **pride,** is a state of mind in which one feels conceited about one's own status, position, and knowledge, based on a self-centered attitude. Regardless of whether one has really achieved something or not, one feels inflated. Someone who has deep pride is very pompous and appears very inflated.

— Next is **ignorance**, which misconceives the identity of the Four Noble Truths, the law of karma, and so forth. In this particular context, ignorance refers to a mental factor that is totally ignorant of the nature of the Three Jewels (the Buddha, his Doctrine, and the Spiritual Community) and the law of karma.

— The delusion of **doubt** is wavering thought concerning whether there are Four Noble Truths or not, whether there is a law of karma or not.

As Tsong-kha-pa (1357–1419), the renowned teacher of Tibetan Buddhism, said, all the realms in which we might take rebirth in the cycle of existence, from the peak of existence to the lowest hell, have the nature of suffering. These sufferings do not come about without any cause, nor are they created by some kind of almighty God. They are products of our own delusions and karmic actions, which are prompted by untamed states of mind.

The root cause of all suffering is the ignorance that misconceives the nature of phenomena and apprehends oneself as self-existent. This ignorance leads us to exaggerate the status of phenomena and create the categories of self and others. These bring about experiences of desire and hatred, which in truth result in all sorts of negative actions. These, in turn, bring about all our undesirable sufferings. If we do not want these sufferings, we should determine whether or not it is possible to get rid of them. If the ignorance that misconceives the self is a mistaken consciousness, it can be eliminated by correcting the mistake. This can be accomplished by generating within our minds a wisdom that realizes the direct opposite of that state of mind, a wisdom realizing that there is no such intrinsically existent self.

When we compare these two states of mind—one believing in an intrinsically existent self and the other perceiving the absence of such a self—the apprehension of self might initially appear very strong and powerful. But because it is a mistaken consciousness, it lacks logical support. The other type of mind, the understanding of selflessness, might be weak at the initial stage, but it has logical support. Sooner or later this wisdom realizing self-lessness is going to gain the upper hand. The truth at the initial stage may not be very obvious, but as we get closer to it, it becomes increasingly self-evident. Something false at the initial stage might seem very solid and firm, but eventually, as we probe it further, it becomes more flimsy and eventually dissolves.

Having seen that all experience in the cycle of existence has a nature of suffering, we should develop a genuine wish to gain liberation from it. Motivated by that wish, we should enter the path of the three trainings: the training of morality, concentration, and wisdom. Among these three, the antidote that will eliminate the delusions is the wisdom realizing selflessness. For that purpose, we first require the mental stability of concentration as the basis, and that in turn depends upon the observance of pure morality. Therefore, we need training in morality as well. At the initial stage, the first priority should be given to the practice of morality; that is the immediate need.

Tsong-kha-pa says that mindfulness and introspection are the foundation of the entire Dharma. In order to have a pure observance of morality, the faculties of introspection and proper mindfulness are required. For laymen and laywomen, the observance of pure morality, refraining from the negative actions, is the foundation of the practice of the path leading to enlightenment. If we do not consider practical needs, like the observance of morality, but instead go in search of more sophisticated practices, our practice will simply be a sham and not really very serious. With the practice of these three trainings—of morality, concentration, and wisdom—we should work for the achievement of liberation not just for ourselves, but also for other sentient beings.

Cyclic Existence

One might wonder, *Since cyclic existence together with its miseries are true sufferings, what is cyclic existence?*

Cyclic existence is divided into three types by way of different types of abodes. These are a *desire realm,* a *form realm,* and a *formless realm.* In the desire realm, beings partake of the pleasures of the "five desirous attributes": forms, sounds, odors, tastes, and tangible objects. The form realm has two parts: In the lower part, beings are not attracted to external pleasures but partake of the pleasures of internal contemplation; in the higher part, beings have turned away from pleasurable feelings altogether and partake of neutral feelings. In the formless realm, all forms, sounds, odors, tastes, and tangible objects, and the five senses for enjoying them, are absent; there is only mind, and beings abide only in neutral feeling, one-pointedly and without distraction.

There are six different types of sentient beings who migrate in cyclic existence: *gods, demigods, humans, hungry ghosts, animals,* and *denizens of hells.* Gods include beings in the form and formless realms, as well as the six types of gods in the desire realm. Demigods are similar to gods but are mischievous and rough. Humans are those of the four "continents" and so forth. Hungry ghosts are many types of beings who are severely deprived of food and drink. Animals are those in the ocean and those scattered about the surface of the earth. Denizens of hells are persons born in various colors and shapes through the force of, and in accordance with, their own previous actions.

The essential meaning of cyclic existence is a process outside of one's control that proceeds in accordance with contaminated actions and afflictions. Its essential nature is misery; its function is to provide a basis for suffering and to induce suffering in the future. Technically, cyclic existence is the contaminated mental and physical aggregates appropriated through contaminated actions and afflictions. Because there is nothing in all three realms to which cyclic existence does not apply, the mental and physical aggregates of all these beings are cyclic existences.

What are the roots of cyclic existence? The sources of suffering are two: contaminated actions and afflictions. Afflictions are classed as peripheral mental factors and are not themselves any of the six main minds (eye, ear, nose, tongue, body, and mental consciousnesses). However, when any of the afflicting mental factors becomes manifest, a main mind (a mental consciousness) comes under its influence, goes wherever the affliction leads it, and "accumulates" a bad action.

There are a great many different kinds of afflictions, but chief among them are desire and hatred. Because of an initial attachment to oneself, hatred arises when something undesirable occurs. Further, through being attached to oneself, the pride that holds one to be superior arises, and similarly when one has no knowledge of something, a wrong view that holds the object of this knowledge to be non-existent arises.

How do self-attachment and so forth arise in such great force? Because of beginningless conditioning, the mind tightly holds to "I" even in dreams, and through the power of this conception, self-attachment and so forth occur. This false conception of "I" arises because of one's lack of knowledge concerning the mode of existence of things. The fact that all objects are empty of inherent existence is obscured, and one conceives things to exist inherently; the strong conception of "I" derives from this. Therefore, the conception that phenomena inherently exist is the afflicting ignorance that is the ultimate root of all afflictions.

Kinds of Actions

From the point of view of their nature, actions are of two types: *intentional* and *operational*. An intentional action occurs prior to physical or verbal deeds and is a mental factor that provides the impulse to act. An operational action is a physical or verbal action that occurs at the time of engaging in activity.

From the point of view of the effects they impel, actions are of three types: *meritorious, non-meritorious,* and *invariable.* Meritorious actions impel one to happy migrations, which are the lives of humans, demigods, and gods. Non-meritorious actions impel one to bad migrations, which are the lives of animals, hungry ghosts, and denizens of hells. Invariable actions impel one to the upper realms, which are those of form and the formless.

All of these can be divided into physical, verbal, and mental actions. Also, from the point of view of the effects that are experienced, actions can be divided into three types: The effects of an action "accumulated" in this life may be experienced in this very life, in the next life, or in any life beyond the next.

As was explained above, the causes of cyclic existence are contaminated actions and afflictions.

If the roots of the afflictions are eliminated and if new actions are not "accumulated," then there are no afflictions to activate the predispositions of contaminated actions persisting from the past, so the causes of cyclic existence have been eliminated.

Then there is freedom from bondage. Some say that as long as one still has mental and physical aggregates wrought by former contaminated actions and afflictions, one has a nirvana with remainder. When these no longer remain, there is a nirvana without remainder. "Without remainder" means that there is no remainder of mental and physical aggregates wrought by contaminated actions and afflictions, but the continuum of consciousness and the continuum of uncontaminated mental and physical aggregates still exist.

By removing the cause, the contaminated aggregates cease, and by becoming free from them all, the suffering that depends on them is extinguished. Such is liberation, of which there are two types: a liberation that is a mere extinguishing of sufferings and their sources; and the great, unsurpassed liberation, the rank of Buddhahood. The former is an extinguishment of all the afflicting obstructions (which prevent liberation from cyclic existence), but not of the obstructions to direct cognition of all objects of knowledge. The latter liberation is the ultimate rank, an utter extinguishing of both the afflictions and the obstruction to omniscience.

The Three Refuges

What are the methods for causing one's own mind to become the practices? Initially, one should take refuge and think about actions and their effects. The refuge is in the *Three Jewels:* the *Buddha,* his *Doctrine,* and the *Spiritual Community.* When a sentient being purifies the taints of his own mind, as well as their latent predispositions, he is free of all defects that act as obstructions. Thus, he simultaneously and directly knows all phenomena. Such a being is called a Buddha, and he is a teacher of refuge, like a physician. The Doctrine jewel is the superior (arya) paths—the chief right paths that remove the taints, as well as his latent predispositions—and the absences that are states of having removed what is to be removed. The Doctrine is the actual refuge, like medicine. The Community jewel is all persons, whether lay or ordained, who have generated a superior path in their continuum. They are friends helping one achieve refuge, like nurses.

Chapter Five

TRANSFORMING
THE MIND

All religions are means, in principle, to help human beings become better, more refined, and more creative. While for certain religions the principal practice is to recite prayers, and for others it is mainly physical penance, in Buddhism the crucial practice is understood to be transforming and improving the mind. This can be viewed in another way. Compared to physical and verbal activities, mental activity is more subtle and difficult to control. Activities of the body and speech are more obvious and easier to learn and practice. In this context, spiritual pursuits involving the mind are more delicate and harder to achieve.

It is essential for us to understand the real meaning of Buddhism. It is very good that interest in Buddhism is growing, but what is more important is to know what Buddhism really is. Unless we understand the essential value and meaning of Buddhist teachings, any attempt to preserve, restore, or propagate them is likely to go off on a wrong track. The doctrine and understanding of the Dharma is not something physical. Therefore, unless it is done with a proper understanding, the mere construction of monasteries or recitation of scriptures may not even be a Dharma practice. The point is that Dharma practice takes place in the mind.

It would be a mistake to think that simply changing our clothes, saying prayers, or making prostrations encompasses the entire practice of the Dharma. Let me explain. When we are making prostrations or circumambulating the temple, all kinds of thoughts arise in our mind.

When you are bored and the day is long, going around the temple can be very pleasant. If you find a talkative friend to accompany you, time just flies. It might make a nice walk, but in a true sense it is not a Dharma practice. There are even occasions when you could apparently be practicing the Dharma, but in reality you are creating negative karma. For instance, a person circumambulating the temple could be devising a plan to deceive someone or plotting revenge against a rival. In his mind he could be saying, *This is how I will get him, this is what I will say, and this is what I will do.* Similarly, you could be reciting holy mantras while your mind indulges in malicious thoughts. Thus, what seems like the physical and verbal practice of the Dharma can prove deceptive.

The Aim of Dharma

We say that the main aim of the practice of the Dharma is to train the mind. How do we do that?

Think about those occasions when you are so angry with someone that you would do anything to hurt him or her. Now to be a proper Dharma practitioner, you need to think rationally about this. You need to think about the numerous defects of anger and the positive results of generating compassion. You can also reflect on the idea that the person who is the object of your anger is just like you in wanting to achieve happiness and get rid of misery. Under such circumstances, how can you justify hurting that person?

You can talk to yourself, saying, "I think of myself as a Buddhist. The moment I open my eyes in the morning, I recite the prayers for taking refuge and developing the awakening mind. I promise to work for all sentient beings, and yet here I am determined to be cruel and unreasonable. How can I call myself a Buddhist? How dare I face the Buddhas when I make a mockery of their part?"

You can completely dissolve your harsh attitude and feelings of anger by thinking in this way. In their place, gentle and kind thoughts can be evoked by reflecting upon how wrong it is to be so angry with that person and how he or she deserves your kindness and goodwill. In this way, you can bring about a true transformation of the heart. This is the Dharma in the true sense of the word. Your previously negative thoughts can be dispelled and replaced by positive and compassionate feelings for that person.

We should note this dramatic change. This is a leap of great significance. It is what is really meant by the practice of the Dharma, but it is not a simple matter.

When the mind is influenced by powerful, virtuous thoughts, no negativity can operate at the same time. If you are motivated by kind and happy thoughts, even seemingly negative actions can bring about positive results. For instance, telling lies is normally negative, but when you do it out of compassion and a rational thought to help someone else, lying can be transformed into something wholesome.

In the Mahayana tradition, the bodhisattva is one who aspires for Buddhahood or enlightenment for the benefit of others. The altruistic thought of the awakening mind stems from the bodhisattva's practice of loving-kindness and compassion. Therefore, on some occasions a bodhisattva is permitted to commit negative physical and verbal actions. Such misdeeds normally give rise to unfavorable results. But depending on the motivation, sometimes these actions can be neutral, and at other times they can become wonderfully meritorious.

These are some reasons why we insist that Buddhism is fundamentally concerned with the mind. Our physical and verbal actions assume only a secondary role. Therefore, the quality or purity of any spiritual practice is determined by the individual's intention and motivation.

Disturbing Emotions

Disturbing emotions are extremely cunning and tough. When a person under their sway is seated on the throne, he is ruled by delusion. As we listen to him talking, his pride swells the longer he carries on. This is how disturbing emotions operate. The effect of disturbing emotions is amazing. They can make a master quarrel with others out of a desire for more students. In such cases, both attachment and animosity are at work.

Fortunately, there is a power that can fight disturbing emotions. It is *wisdom*. This wisdom becomes clearer and sharper when we apply analysis and examination. It is forceful and enduring. On the other hand, the ignorant mind, although it can be cunning, cannot withstand analysis. Under intelligent examination, it collapses. Understanding this gives us confidence to tackle the problems created by disturbing emotions. If we study and reflect, we can gain a good understanding of wisdom and of disturbing emotions like hostility and attachment, which are produced by the mind that believes that things are true, that they exist as they appear.

The mind conceiving of true existence is extremely active, forceful, and crafty. Its close companion,the self-centered attitude, is equally hardy and willful. For too long we have been thoroughly under its power. It has posed as our friend, support, and protector. Now, if we are careful and judicious, we should develop the wisdom that understands that things do not exist as they appear, that they lack this type of truth; this is called the wisdom of emptiness. By employing this weapon with sustained effort, we will have the chance to fight back against disturbing emotions.

Now the defects we are referring to are the sources of suffering: karma and disturbing emotions, as well as the imprints left by them. These defects can be removed only by applying appropriate antidotes. The imprints left by disturbing emotions obstruct individuals from gaining omniscience. Consciousness by its very nature has the potential to know everything, but these defects veil and obstruct the mind from such knowledge. Eliminating these obstructions by developing the necessary opponents is accomplished by the mind. When consciousness is totally free from obstruction, it automatically becomes fully aware, and that person awakens to full enlightenment.

The state of enlightenment is not some kind of physical entity like a heavenly abode. It is the intrinsic quality of the mind revealed in its full positive potential. Therefore, in order to reach this state of awakening, the practitioner has to begin by eliminating the negativities of the mind and developing positive qualities one by one. It is the mind that actively applies the antidote in the process of removing the negative impulses and obscurations. There comes a point when disturbing emotions and mental obstructions can never recur, no matter what happens.

By the same token, it is the mind that is exclusively involved in developing spiritual insight and knowledge. However small the positive energy may be to begin with, in due course the mind becomes fully consummated with knowledge and awakens to Buddhahood.

It is important to remember that all that the Buddha taught was meant to help sentient beings and guide them on the spiritual path. His philosophical teachings were not just abstract speculation, but part of the processes and techniques for combating disturbing emotions. We can appreciate the appropriateness of the antidotes for different disturbing emotions from our own experience. The Buddha taught that to counter anger and hatred we should meditate on loving-kindness. Paying attention to an object's repulsive side serves to defeat attachment to the object. There is much logical reasoning to show that the appearance of true existence is a mistake. The conception of true existence is an ignorant one, and the wisdom realizing emptiness is its direct opponent.

From such teachings, we can infer that disturbing emotions are only temporary afflictions of the mind and that they can be completely eradicated. When the mind is free of defilements, the potential of its true nature—clarity and awareness—is fully revealed. As the understanding of this is enriched, the practitioner comes to appreciate the possibility of attaining nirvana and Buddhahood. This comes as a wonderful revelation.

Even if all the gods in the universe joined forces against you, if every living being became hostile toward you, they would not have the power to send you to hell. Disturbing emotions, on the other hand, can deliver you to hell in a single instant. This is why disturbing emotions have been our enemy from beginningless time, harming and destroying us. There has never been an enemy so enduring as these disturbing emotions. Ordinary enemies die and disappear. If you comply with the wishes of an ordinary enemy, gradually he or she will become your friend. Your enemy will become someone who brings you benefit. In the case of disturbing emotions, the more you rely on them, the more they will harm you and bring suffering to you. They have been our constant enemy, the sole cause of all our sufferings. As long as we let this enemy reside peacefully with us, we will have no happiness.

When you wage a war with an ordinary enemy, you might gain victory and drive the enemy from your country. Ordinary enemies can regroup, reinforce, and reequip themselves and return to the battle. But when you fight disturbing emotions, once you have defeated and eliminated them, they cannot return. From this perspective, disturbing emotions are weak; we do not need nuclear missiles or bombs to destroy them. They are weak because once we are able to see reality and cultivate the eye of wisdom, we can remove disturbing emotions. And once we destroy the disturbing emotions within our minds, where will they go? They disappear into emptiness. They cannot reappear somewhere else and reinforce themselves, so they cannot return to harm us.

There is no disturbing emotion that has independent existence. When attachment and anger arise within our minds, they are quite powerful and leave our minds disturbed. Even so, on closer scrutiny, they have no special place to hide. They do not abide in the body, nor do they abide in our sense faculties.

If you try to find disturbing emotions among the collection of mental and physical components, or outside them, you will not find them there. Disturbing emotions are like an illusion. Why should we let them plunge us into hell?

Maintaining Mindfulness

Both positive and negative experiences arise from the mind, depending on whether your mind is transformed or not. Therefore, it is most important to control and discipline the mind.

All the fears and the immeasurable sufferings that we encounter arise from the mind. The Buddha taught that there is no enemy more powerful than the mind. In all the realms of existence, there is nothing more frightful—nothing more to be feared—than the mind. Likewise, he said that the disciplined mind gives rise to all excellent qualities. The source and cause of peace and happiness is the mind. Happiness arises from virtuous practice; sufferings arise from negative practice.

So happiness and suffering depend upon whether your mind is transformed or not. Even in the short term, the more you control and discipline your mind, the happier and more relaxed you will be.

Once the mind within is controlled and relaxed, even if the whole universe appears to turn on you like an enemy, you will not feel threatened or unhappy. On the other hand, if you are internally disturbed and agitated, even if the most delicious food is laid out on the table in front of you, you will not enjoy it. You may hear pleasant things, but they will bring you no joy. So, depending on whether your mind is disciplined or not, you will experience happiness or suffering.

Once you transform your mind so that you have no possessiveness and no craving, you will achieve the perfection of giving. The perfection of giving means that you offer everything that you have, as well as the positive results of that offering, to all sentient beings. The practice is entirely dependent on the mind. The perfection of ethics is similar. Achieving the perfection of ethics means that you attain a state of mind that refrains from harming sentient beings in any way at all. It is a state completely free from self-centeredness. The practice of patience is the same. Unruly sentient beings are as infinite as the extent of space. However, once you control your own mind, it is as if you have destroyed all external enemies. If your mind is calm, even though the whole environment is hostile, you will not be disturbed. To protect your feet from thorns, you cannot cover the entire surface of the earth with leather.

If you want to protect the mind, you must make an effort to maintain mindfulness. When you do not pay attention and your mindfulness degenerates, the merit you accumulated in the past will be lost as if it had been stolen by thieves. Consequently, you will fall into an unfavorable state of existence. Disturbing emotions are like robbers and thieves: They are always alert, looking for an opportunity. If they find it, they take it and rob you of virtue. They take the life of our happy existence. Therefore, never allow your mindfulness to weaken. If you occasionally lose your mindfulness, restore it by remembering the endless sufferings in the cycle of existence.

What are the methods of maintaining mindfulness and alertness? To associate with spiritual teachers and to listen to teachings, to know what is to be practiced and what is to be given up. The more respect you have for the teachings, the more careful you will be. When you associate with good friends, you will remain naturally alert. You can discover what is to be given up and what is to be practiced by listening to the teachings and following the example of good friends. When you reflect on explanations of the nature of impermanence and the sufferings of the cycle of existence, you will cultivate fear within your mind. Because of such fear, a fortunate person will quickly be able to be mindful.

The other method for cultivating mindfulness is to remember that Buddhas and bodhisattvas possess an omniscient mind. They constantly know what you are doing; when you remember their presence, you will be more careful. You will be ashamed if you do something negative.

Since the Buddhas and bodhisattvas possess unobstructed awareness, we cannot hide anything from them. Understanding this and remaining respectful is the practice of recollecting the Buddhas. Normally, we tend to think that the Buddhas and bodhisattvas will pay attention to us only if we recite some prayer or invocation or call them by name. This is a mistake. The Buddha's omniscient mind pervades everything, even the subtlest particles. In other words, the Buddha's mind is aware of all phenomena, regardless of time and place.

Understanding that you are always in the presence of the omniscient Buddhas is the way to recollect the Buddha and his qualities. This is very important for your daily practice.

If you are mindful, when one of these defects is about to arise, you will be able to restrain yourself. For example, it may be that while you are talking to someone, you begin to get angry. Your mindfulness will prompt you either to stop the conversation or to change the subject. Think to yourself that even though the other person is being unreasonable and using provocative words, there is no use retaliating in kind. Instead of dwelling on this situation, turn your mind to the other person's good points. This will also help reduce your anger.

The elephantine mind is intoxicated by disturbing emotions, so you should bind it to the great pillar of spiritual practice. With all your effort, examine your mind and try not to let it wander even for a moment. Watch what it is about to do and what it is doing. When you are about to meditate, for example, at the outset you must cultivate an intention to be careful and not let yourself be distracted. As a result, you may be successful in meditating for about 15 minutes without being distracted. Once you get used to it, you can lengthen the session.

Of course, it is difficult to control the mind and make it stay on the object of meditation. It is difficult to make your mind do what you want it to, but as you gradually get used to it, you will achieve some success. You can employ whatever techniques help you control your mind. For example, you might find that sitting facing a wall helps you control your distractions when you are doing certain meditations. Sometimes closing your eyes may help. At other times keeping them open may be of more help. It depends on your personal inclination and your circumstances.

This is how you can always be alert and guard against disturbing emotions and getting involved in meaningless activity. If you want to go somewhere or you want to say something, first determine whether it is proper or not. When attachment is about to arise within you or you feel like getting angry with someone, do not do anything: Do not speak; do not think—remain like a piece of wood.

If you find yourself inclined to break into meaningless laughter, you want to brag about something, you want to discuss the faults of others, you want to deceive others, you want to say something improper or make sarcastic remarks, or you want to praise yourself and criticize or scold others, at that time remain like a piece of wood. If you find you want to obtain possessions, respect, fame, and renown; or you want to gather a coterie of followers around you, remain like a piece of wood. If you find that you are inclined to neglect the purposes of others but aspire to fulfill your own—and, what is more, you want to talk about it—remain like a piece of wood. When you are inclined to become impatient, lazy, or despondent; or you want to make presumptuous remarks; or you are inclined to become self-satisfied, remain like a piece of wood.

Remain alert and become skillful in what is to be practiced and what is to be given up. Have the confidence to engage in positive activities without simply depending on other people for their support. Do not give up a major practice for the sake of a minor practice. The most important thing is that whatever you do should benefit other people; it should have the effect of fulfilling the wishes of other people.

Having understood this crucial point, we should make constant efforts on behalf of other people. This is what the compassionate Buddha has taught. The Buddha was farsighted and knew what would be useful in the long term and what would be useful in the short term. This is why his advice is flexible, and a bodhisattva who constantly works for the benefit of others is sometimes permitted to do things that are normally prohibited.

It is the nature of the mind that the better acquainted it becomes with doing something, the easier that thing is to do. If we are able to view suffering from a transformed perspective, we will be able to tolerate even greater levels of suffering. There is nothing that does not become easier with familiarity. If we get used to putting up with minor hurts, we will gradually develop tolerance for greater pain.

We see many people who put up with being attacked by insects, with the discomfort of hunger and thirst, with being pricked and scratched by thorns as they go about their daily life. People face all such meaningless sufferings easily once they get used to them. Therefore, when we encounter minor problems due to heat and cold, wind and rain, sickness and injury, to fret will only make the problem worse. Some people, instead of being frightened at the sight of their own blood, become even more courageous. Others, at the sight of any blood, let alone their own, fall down in a faint. The difference arises because people have different degrees of mental stability. Some are resolute, others quite cowardly.

If you voluntarily learn to face minor problems, you will gradually become invincible to the different levels of suffering. It is the way of the wise that, faced with suffering, they never allow their minds to become disturbed.

Through the gates of the five sense organs a being sees, hears, smells, tastes, and comes into contact with a host of external forms, objects, and impressions. Let the form, sound, smell, taste, touch, and mental events, which are the relations of the six senses, be shut off. When this is done, the recollection of past events on which the mind tends to dwell will be completely discontinued and the flow of memory cut off. Similarly, plans for the future and contemplation of future action must not be allowed to arise. It is necessary to create a vacuum in place of all such processes of thought. Freed from all these processes, there will remain a pure, clean, distinct, and quiescent mind.

᭞᭞᭞

Chapter Six

HOW TO MEDITATE

The essence of Buddhist teachings can be summarized as the view of interdependence coupled with the conduct of nonviolence. These are the fundamentals I want you to remember. There is no functional phenomenon that exists independently or on its own. All phenomena depend on other factors. Things are interdependent. For example, peace in one nation depends on the attitude of its neighboring countries and the general security in the world. The happiness of one family depends on its neighbors and society at large. Buddhists believe in the theory of dependent origination, not in an almighty creator or in production from no cause at all.

When people forget basic ethical principles and act with a selfish attitude, unpleasant consequences ensue. When you think that your neighbors have nothing to do with your own happiness, you mistreat them. You bully some of them and intimidate and curse others. Can you expect an atmosphere of peace and harmony in such a neighborhood? The answer is obviously no. When you entertain evil thoughts like hostility and hatred, there is no joy in your heart and you are a nuisance to others. On the other hand, if you develop kindness, patience, and understanding, then the whole atmosphere changes. Our text, the Seven-Point Mind Training, says: First train in the preliminaries.

There are four preliminary practices: thinking about the rarity and potential of life as a free and fortunate human being, reflecting on death and impermanence, thinking about actions and their results, and reflecting on the faults of the cycle of existence. For example, by reflecting on the rarity and potential of life as a free and fortunate human being, you overcome your obsession with the temporal pleasures of this life. By contemplating death and impermanence, you overcome your attraction to favorable rebirths in future lives.

Now, different activities are to be performed during the actual meditation session and during the post-meditation periods. We normally try to concentrate as much as possible during the meditation. If after meditating we leave the mind unguarded and distracted, it will harm our progress. Therefore, post-meditation practices are recommended.

Meditation means creating a continual familiarity with a virtuous object in order to transform your mind. Merely understanding some point does not transform your mind. You may intellectually see the advantages of an altruistic awakening mind, but that does not actually affect your self-centered attitude. Your self-centeredness will be dispelled only through constantly familiarizing yourself with that understanding. That is what is meant by meditation.

Meditation can be of two types: *Analytical meditation* uses analysis and reflection, whereas in *single-pointed meditation* the mind dwells on whatever has been understood. When you meditate on love and compassion, you try to cultivate such an attitude in your mind, thinking, *May all sentient beings be free from suffering.* On the other hand, when you meditate on emptiness or impermanence, you take impermanence or emptiness as the object of your meditation.

Here in the practice of mind training, we require preliminary practices like meditation on death and impermanence to urge us into doing the main practice.

When you do these meditations, analyze the topic first. Once you have come to a certain conclusion, retain it in your mind and concentrate on it for some time. When you find that you are losing your concentration, again employ analysis. You can carry on with the same round of meditation again and again until you see some kind of effect within your mind. Then, change the pattern of reasons you employ, as outlined in ancient texts like the Guide to the Bodhisattva's Way of Life, the Precious Garland, and so forth.

This is like trying out different medicines: You may find that some medicines work better than others. If you just go on stubbornly sticking to one round of meditation, it may not be very helpful. You have to put in a lot of effort. This is why study is necessary. Meditation without prior study is like someone trying to climb a rocky cliff without hands.

Posture and Breathing

Before I explain the correct posture and breathing technique for meditation, I would like to touch upon the correct environment for your practice. For the beginner, the setting in which meditation takes place is important. Once we have developed certain experiences, then external factors have very little effect. But generally speaking, the place for meditation should be quiet. When we meditate on single-pointedness of mind, then we need a completely isolated place, one with no noise.

It is equally important to clean the environment in which you are performing the meditation. You clean it not just for mundane reasons, but also to induce a psychological effect of greater mental clarity. As Po-to-wa, one of Atisha's principal disciples, said, "Once a meditator has reached an advanced level, every action that he performs can become a stimulus for his practice." So, when you clean the place, think of it as a reminder that what actually has to be cleaned is the mind.

To maintain the correct physical posture during meditation, the meditation seat should be slightly raised at the back, because that helps reduce tightness. Sitting in *vajra* (cross-legged) position is very difficult, but if it causes no pain, then that is the proper way. Or you can sit in half vajra or in Arya Tara's posture (right leg extended out, left leg folded in a meditative posture), which is very comfortable.

In the correct hand *mudra,* or gesture, the back of the right hand rests in the palm of the left hand, and the two thumbs stand up and touch one another, forming a triangle. The triangle has a tantric significance, symbolizing the realm of truth, the reality source, and also inner heat at the navel.

The arms should not touch the body. The head is slightly bent down, the tip of the tongue touching the palate, which prevents thirst and drooling when the meditator engages in deep, single-pointed concentration. Lips and teeth should be left in their natural position, eyes looking at the tip of the nose. As for the position of the eyes, at the beginning it might give you a clearer visualization when they are closed, but in the long run this is not good; you should not close your eyes. Visualization is done on a mental and not a sensory level. If you train yourself to meditate with open eyes, you will not lose the mental image you are meditating on. On the other hand, if you train yourself and become used to meditating with closed eyes, you will lose the mental image the moment you open them.

During meditation, your breathing should be natural. You should not breathe violently or too gently. When you are in a fluctuating state of mind, like when you are angry or have lost your temper, then it is good to bring back calmness by concentrating on breathing. Just count the breaths, completely forgetting about anger. Concentrate on breathing and count in/out "1, 2, 3," up to 20. At that moment when your mind concentrates fully on breathing, the breath coming and going, the passions subside. Afterward it is easier to think clearly.

Since all activities, including meditation, depend very much on the force of intention or motivation, it is important that before you begin to meditate, you cultivate a correct motivation. However, motivation should not be influenced by the concern for perfection and happiness of the samsaric life alone. The correct motivation is the altruistic attitude.

Abiding in Calm

In developing a meditation practice, one must progress in the training of meditative stabilization, which is the mind's abiding one-pointedly on its object. There are many types of meditative stabilization, but let us explain calm abiding *(shamatha)* here. The nature of calm abiding is the one-pointed abiding on any object, without distraction, of a mind conjoined with a bliss of physical and mental pliancy. If it is supplemented with taking refuge, it is a Buddhist practice, and if it is supplemented with an aspiration to highest enlightenment for the sake of all sentient beings, it is a Mahayana practice.

Its merits are that if one has achieved calm abiding, one's mind and body are pervaded by joy and bliss: One can—through the power of its mental and physical pliancy—set the mind on any virtuous object one chooses, and many special qualities such as clairvoyance and emanations are attained. The main purpose and advantage of calm abiding are that through it, one can achieve special insight *(vipasyana)*, which realizes emptiness, and can thereby be liberated from cyclic existence.

One should have all the following causal collections for the achievement of calm abiding. The place where one practices should be free of noise, since noise is a thorn to concentration: The area and water should be congenial. The meditator himself should have few wants, know satisfaction, be free from the din and bustle of the world, and should avoid nonvirtuous physical and verbal deeds. Through hearing and thinking, he should have eliminated misconceptions about the subjects of meditation; he should know how to reflect on the faults of desire, on the meaning of impermanence, and so on.

With regard to the actual practice of calm abiding, Maitreya Bodhisattva, the future Buddha, says in his Discrimination of the Middle Way and the Extremes (Madhyantavibhanga): The cause of its arising is to observe the relinquishing of the five faults and the application of the eight antidotes.

The five faults to be relinquished are:

- **Laziness:** not wishing to cultivate meditative stabilization

- **Forgetfulness:** not remembering the object of meditation

- **Lethargy and excitement:** interruptions of meditative stabilization

- **Non-application of the antidotes:** occurring when lethargy and excitement arise

- **Overapplication:** continuing to apply the antidotes even though lethargy and excitement have been extinguished

The eight antidotes are the means for relinquishing these faults. The antidotes to laziness are:

- **Faith:** seeing the good qualities of meditative stabilization

- **Aspiration:** seeking to attain those good qualities

- **Effort:** delighting in engaging in meditative stabilization

- **Physical and mental pliancy:** an effect (of effort)

The antidote to forgetfulness is:

- **Mindfulness:** maintaining concentration on an object continuously

The antidote to lethargy and excitement is:

- **Awareness:** knowing that lethargy or excitement has arisen or is arising

The antidote to non-application is:

- **Application:** engaging in the antidotes to lethargy or excitement

The antidote to overapplication is:

- **Desisting from application:** relaxing one's effort

States of Concentration

Through applying the eight antidotes, the five faults are gradually eliminated and one passes through nine states of concentration, which are:

- **Setting the mind:** collecting the mind and aiming it at an internal object (such as the visualized form of the Buddha)

- **Continually setting:** prolonging concentration on the object more than in the previous state

- **Resetting:** immediately recognizing distraction and returning to the object

- **Increased setting:** collecting the mind from concentrating on the gross (aspects of the visualized object of meditation),

and setting it more and more steadily on
the subtle (details of the object)

- **Disciplining:** knowing the good qualities of meditative stabilization and taking
joy in them

- **Pacifying:** ceasing dislike for meditative
stabilization

- **Thorough pacifying:** through effort,
relinquishing even subtle lethargy and
excitement just after they arise

- **Making one-pointed:** generating meditative stabilization continuously within
the context of it being impossible for the
non-conducive to interrupt the process

- **Putting in equipoise:** spontaneously fixing on the object of meditation without
requiring the effort of relying on mindfulness and awareness

The above nine states of concentration are accomplished by means of the six powers. The first state
is accomplished through the power of hearing, the

second through the power of thinking, and the third and fourth through the power of mindfulness. The fifth and sixth are accomplished through the power of familiarity.

The periods of the four mental activities (which are ways in which the mind engages its object) occur during the nine states of concentration:

- **Forcibly fixing:** during the first and second states, the mind is strenuously fixed on its object of concentration

- **Interruptedly fixing:** from the third to the seventh state, concentration occurs intermittently

- **Non-interruptedly fixing:** during the eighth state, the mind is capable of staying on its object without interruption

- **Effortlessly fixing:** during the ninth state, the mind spontaneously remains on its object

If one knows the nature, order, and distinctions of the levels explained above without error and cultivates calm abiding, one can easily generate faultless meditative stabilization in about a year.

This has been a treatment of the topic of calm abiding that applies to objects in general. In particular, if one cultivates calm abiding taking the mind itself as the object, additional advantages are found. One identifies one's own mind. The mind is as vacuous as space, not having any physical qualities such as form or shape. It is something that merely perceives whatever aspects of an object appear to it with vivid clarity. Once the mind has been identified to be like this, one then engages in the time state, the relinquishing of the five faults, the application of the eight antidotes, and so forth, as has been explained above. One thus cultivates calm abiding.

This has been a mere enumeration of the elements of calm abiding in the sense of my having made an extreme abbreviation of early Buddhist teachings. The measure of having achieved calm abiding is that once physical and then mental pliancy have been achieved, one attains a pliancy of immovability, which is the mind's abiding one-pointedly on its object. At that time, one achieves an actual calm abiding, which is included in the preparation stage for the first concentration. Of the three realms, this concentration belongs to the form realm. Having attained calm abiding, the mind is serviceable, and no matter on what type of virtuous object or meaning it is set, the mind remains there one-pointedly. Through the force of this, the ability of the mind to comprehend a meaning is very great.

Chapter Seven

THE AWAKENING MIND

The awakening mind is the intention to achieve Buddhahood in order to free all beings in the universe from suffering. In order to develop the awakening mind, we must meditate; it cannot be cultivated merely by wishful thinking and prayers. It cannot be cultivated merely by gaining an intellectual understanding of what it means. Nor can it be cultivated simply by receiving blessings. We have to cultivate it through meditation and repeated and prolonged habituation. In order to be able to sustain meditation on the awakening mind, we need to first appreciate the benefits of its cultivation. We need to develop an intense longing to cultivate the awakening mind, seeing it as a pressing need.

It is thus obvious that it is worthwhile to cultivate a good heart, but the question is how to go about it. When it comes to training the mind, a good heart refers to the awakening mind, which is the best, supreme, and ultimate mode of the good heart. It is an unlimited good mind complemented by wisdom. The scriptures explain that the awakening mind is a mind with two aspirations: an aspiration to fulfill the purposes of others, assisted by an aspiration to achieve Buddhahood.

Now, what do we mean when we say "complemented by wisdom"? Let us take the case of a mind taking refuge in the Buddha. Such a state of mind might involve accepting that the Buddha is an ultimate object of refuge free from all faults and possessing all qualities. It could simply be accepting that the Buddha is a precious and holy being. It could be a matter of faith.

But there is also another process of taking refuge based on analysis and inquiry regarding the nature of such a Buddha and the possibility of his or her existence. As a result of such an examination, we can come to understand that such a Buddha is possible. We come to understand the nature of the Buddha, that he or she possesses a mind with unique qualities free from all obstructions. And having understood the meaning of such a superior Buddha, we can cultivate a deep sense of taking refuge in the Buddha based on conviction. This is much stronger and more stable than mere faith.

Cultivating the awakening mind is similar to this. It is possible for there to be a bodhisattva who has not understood emptiness yet, but at the same time has a wholehearted aspiration to fulfill the purposes and wishes of sentient beings. Based on that aspiration, he or she could generate a mind aspiring to Buddhahood for the sake of all sentient beings. But usually when we talk about the awakening mind, it is based on investigating whether the sufferings of infinite sentient beings can be eliminated and, if so, determining the means for doing so. Based on such reflections and thoughts, we examine the meaning of enlightenment, as stated in the following lines:

Compassion focusing on sentient beings.
And wisdom focusing on enlightenment.

When we cultivate the noble awakening mind wishing to achieve enlightenment for the sake of sentient beings, augmented by the knowledge that enlightenment can be achieved, it becomes a wonderful and courageous mind.

When we train in the awakening mind, we should train in these two aspirations—the aspiration toward Buddhahood and the aspiration wishing to benefit others. The source of the aspiration to benefit others, the awakening mind that has greater concern for others than oneself, is compassion. In the course of cultivating genuine compassion, we train in the mind that has a strong concern for sentient beings afflicted by suffering, and in the mind that views suffering sentient beings as pleasing and lovable. But at the same time we should be able to see the nature of the sufferings by which these sentient beings are afflicted. We should train in these two separately.

The Seed of Buddhahood

The only entrance to the path of the Great Vehicle (Mahayana Buddhism) is the generation of the awakening mind. Within the Great Vehicle there are only two vehicles, the sutra vehicle and the tantra vehicle. Whichever you wish to enter, the only entrance is with the awakening mind. When you possess the awakening mind, you belong to the Great Vehicle, but as soon as you give it up, you fall away from it. The moment you generate the awakening mind, even if you are bound in the sufferings of the cycle of existence, you will become an object of respect even for the Buddhas, who are themselves awakened.

Just as a fragment of a diamond is an excellent jewel that surpasses all other ornaments, the diamond-like awakening mind, even when it is weak, outshines all the qualities possessed by those pursuing personal liberation. Nagarjuna, the Buddhist philosopher, says in the Precious Garland that if you wish to attain the unsurpassable state of supreme enlightenment, its source is the awakening mind. Therefore, generate an awakening mind as stable as the king of mountains.

Those who have not developed the awakening mind cannot enter into the secret practice of tantra. Access to tantric teachings is restricted to those who have received initiation and empowerment, and if you do not possess the awakening mind, you cannot receive tantric initiation. This is a clear statement that entrance to the secret vehicle also depends on possessing the awakening mind.

The awakening mind is like a seed for the attainment of Buddhahood. It is like a field in which to cultivate all positive qualities. It is like the ground on which everything rests. It is like the god of wealth who removes all poverty. It is like a father protecting all bodhisattvas. It is like a wish-fulfilling jewel. It is like a miraculous vase fulfilling all your wishes. It is like a spear vanquishing the foe of disturbing emotions. It is like armor shielding you from improper thoughts. It is like a sword beheading the disturbing emotions. It is like a weapon staving off all kinds of attacks. It is like a hook to draw you out of the waters of the cycle of existence. It is like the whirlwind that scatters all mental obstacles and their sources. It is like the concentrated teaching encompassing all the bodhisattvas' prayers and activities. It is like a shrine before which everyone can make offerings.

Therefore, having found this precious life as a free and fortunate human being, and having come across the complete teachings of the Buddha, we should treasure the awakening mind. What makes the Tibetan Buddhist tradition so valuable is that it includes precious techniques for generating the awakening mind. The existence of this tradition of cultivating love and compassion and developing concern for the welfare of other sentient beings is extremely fortunate. I myself feel extremely fortunate to be able to explain such teachings at times like these. Likewise, you are extremely fortunate to be able to read about such an invaluable attitude.

We should not think of the awakening mind merely as an object of admiration, something to pay respect to. It is something we should generate within ourselves. We have the ability and option to do so.

You may have been a horribly selfish person in the earlier part of your life, but with determination you can transform your mind. You may become like the person described in a prayer, who "never expects to work for her own purpose, but always works for the benefit of others."

Tools for Developing an Awakening Mind

As human beings, we have intelligence and courage. Provided we use these attributes, we will be able to achieve what we set out to do. I personally have no experience of the awakening mind, but when I was in my 30s, I used to reflect on the Four Noble Truths and compare the possibility of attaining liberation and developing the awakening mind. I used to think that attaining liberation for myself was possible. But when I thought about the awakening mind, it seemed quite far off. I used to think that even though it was a marvelous quality, it would be really difficult to achieve.

Time has passed, and even though I still have not developed the awakening mind, I feel quite close to it. Now I think that if I work hard enough, I may be able to develop it. Hearing and thinking about the awakening mind makes me feel happy and sad at the same time. Like everyone else, I, too, experience negative emotions like anger, jealousy, and competitiveness, but due to repeated familiarity, I also feel that I am getting closer to the awakening mind. It is a unique quality of the mind that once you get familiar with a particular object, your mind gains stability in relation to it. Unlike physical progress, which is subject to natural restrictions, the qualities of the mind can be developed limitlessly. The mind is like a fire, which, if you continually feed it, will grow further. There is nothing that does not get easier with familiarity.

The first step in actually developing the conventional awakening mind, which is concerned with the interests of others, is to appreciate the faults of self-centeredness and the advantages of cherishing others. A principal practice for developing this awakening mind is the practice of exchanging oneself with others. There are different explanations about how to engage in this practice. In all the explanations, one factor is common: It is necessary at the outset to regard sentient beings with affection. We should think of them as pleasing and attractive and try to cultivate a strong sense of affection for them. This requires generating a sense of equanimity that regulates our fluctuating emotions toward other sentient beings.

To do this, it is very helpful to visualize three people in front of you: one who is your relative or friend, another who is an enemy, and someone toward whom you feel neutral. Observe your natural reaction to them. Usually we are predisposed to feeling close to our relatives, distant from our enemies, and indifferent to everyone else. When you think about your friend, you feel close to her and immediately have a sense of concern for her welfare. When you think about your enemy, you immediately feel uncomfortable and ill at ease. You might even be pleased if he were to run into difficulties. When you think about the person toward whom you feel neutral, you find you do not really care whether that person is miserable or happy. You feel indifferent. When you recognize such fluctuating emotions, ask yourself whether they are justified. If you imagine your friend doing you harm, you will find that your reaction to her will change.

Those whom we call our friends in this present life have not been our friends forever. Neither have those we presently think of as enemies been hostile forever. This person who is a friend or relative in this lifetime could have been our enemy in a past lifetime. Similarly, the person whom we regard as an enemy now could have been one of our parents in a previous life. Therefore, it is foolish only to be concerned about those we think of now as friends and to disregard those we think of as enemies.

The aim here is to reduce attachment toward your relatives and friends, while reducing anger and hatred toward your enemies. Reflect upon the notion that there is no sentient being who has not been your friend. This is how you cultivate equanimity toward all other sentient beings.

It is also only in relation to other sentient beings that we can observe pure ethics, such as abstaining from killing, stealing, and sexual abuse. None of the ten virtuous actions can be undertaken except in relation to other sentient beings. Similarly, we can cultivate the practice of generosity, ethics, and patience only in relation to other sentient beings. Only in relation to them can we develop love, compassion, and the awakening mind. Compassion, for example, is a state of mind that comes about when we focus on the sufferings of other sentient beings and cultivate a strong wish that they be free from such sufferings. Therefore, without other sentient beings as the object, we would be unable to cultivate compassion.

The mind cannot be transformed by force, using knives and guns. It may seem to be weak, having no color or shape, but it is actually tough and resilient. The only way to change it is by using the mind itself. For only the mind can distinguish between what is to be done and what is to be given up. This is how the darkness of ignorance can be dispelled. When the mind can see the temporary and ultimate benefits of engaging in virtue and the faults of nonvirtuous misdeeds, we will then be able to act accordingly.

Generating love and compassion is extremely important for your practice in the beginning, in the middle, and in the end when you attain Buddha-hood. And it is only by attaining the fully awakened state of a Buddha that you have the capacity to fulfill the purposes of sentient beings. Practices like the four means of gathering disciples (giving, speaking pleasantly, teaching, and acting in accordance with the teachings) and the six perfections (generosity, discipline, patience, effort, concentration, and wisdom) are actually generated in dependence on sentient beings. All the fruitful practices of the Great Vehicle arise in relation to the concern for the

welfare of other sentient beings. Therefore, whenever your gaze falls upon a sentient being, thinking,
I shall fully awaken by depending on such beings as this,
behold her with love and compassion.

Just as you will be able to harvest good crops if
you plant healthy seeds in fertile soil, by cherishing sentient beings you will reap the fine crop of
Buddhahood. By cherishing the welfare of sentient
beings, you will be able to attain both good rebirth
and the full awakening of a Buddha. The many types
of suffering experienced by animals, hungry spirits,
and the inhabitants of hell are the result of harming
sentient beings. Neglecting the welfare of sentient
beings, you will encounter the miseries of eating and
being eaten by others, hunger and thirst, and overwhelming and unrelenting pain.

Giving and taking is a practice that should be
undertaken with great mental courage and determination. The great Buddhist teacher Sha-ra-wa
(1070–1141) said that if you really want to accustom your mind to such an instruction, your practice
should not be merely like a stone tumbling down a
steep slope, nor should it be like lukewarm water in a
stagnant pool. It should be red as blood and white as
curd. This means that to train your mind you should
not be halfhearted, hesitant, or apprehensive, but

totally dedicated and decisive. You cannot expect to engage in the practice of mind training one day and the next day do something else, if you are looking for success.

Having trained in love and compassion, you might wonder why you need to attain the fully awakened state of a Buddha. The great beings intent on personal liberation and bodhisattvas on the tenth level of spiritual development have a great capacity to help other beings. However, only by attaining complete enlightenment can they place innumerable beings in the state beyond suffering. Therefore, you should generate a strong aspiration to attain the fully awakened state of a Buddha, capable of fulfilling both your own and others' purposes.

Nowadays, many of us might doubt whether it is really possible to reach the state of Buddhahood. When we talk about Buddhahood, we might think only of Buddha Shakyamuni, who appeared in this world just over 2,500 years ago. Therefore, it is important to have a good understanding of the nature of enlightenment. First, we have to understand the possibility of removing the faults that contaminate our minds. This is what makes the attainment of enlightenment possible. If we can understand that, it will inspire our efforts to generate the awakening mind. Therefore, it is said that wisdom focuses on enlightenment and compassion focuses on the needs of other sentient beings. Once we appreciate the possibility of attaining enlightenment within our own minds, we will aspire to achieve it.

Seven-Point Mind Training

This is the work written by the Buddhist teacher Geshe Chekawa (1101–1175) as a result of his long experience in teaching the practice of mind training:

Homage to great compassion.
The essence of this nectar of secret instruction
Is transmitted from the master from Sumatra.
You should understand the significance of this
    instruction
As like a diamond, the sun, and a medicinal
    tree.
This time of the five degenerations will then
    be transformed
Into the path to the fully awakened state.

1. Explaining the Preliminaries as a Basis for the Practice

First, train in the preliminaries.

2. (a) The Actual Practice: Training in the Conventional Awakening Mind

Banish the one to blame for everything.
Meditate on the great kindness of all sentient
    beings.
Practice a combination of giving and taking.
Giving and taking should be practiced
    alternately
And you should begin by taking from yourself.
These two should be made to ride on the
    breath.
Concerning the three objects, three poisons,
    and three virtues
The instruction to be followed, in brief,
Is to take these words to heart in all activities.

(b) Training in the Ultimate
Awakening Mind

When stability has been attained, impart the
     secret teaching:
Consider all phenomena as like dreams,
Examine the nature of unborn awareness.
The remedy itself is released in its own place,
Place the essence of the path on the nature of
     the basis of all.
In between meditation sessions, be like a
     conjuror, a creator of illusions.

3. Transforming Adverse Circumstances
into the Path to Enlightenment

When the environment and its inhabitants
     overflow with unwholesomeness
Transform adverse circumstances into the path
     to enlightenment.
Reflect immediately at every opportunity.
The supreme method is accompanied by the
     four practices.

4. The Integrated Practice
of a Single Lifetime

Train in the five powers.
The five powers themselves are the
    Great Vehicle's
Precept on the transference of consciousness.
Cultivate these paths of practice.

5. The Measure of Having
Trained the Mind

Integrate all the teachings into one thought.
Primary importance should be given to the
    two witnesses.
Constantly cultivate only a joyful mind.
The measure of a trained mind is that it has
    turned back.
There are five great marks of a trained mind.
The trained (mind) retains control even
    when distracted.

6. The Commitments of Mind Training

Always train in the three general points.
Engage vigorously in forceful means to cultivate
    qualities and abandon disturbing emotions.
Subjugate all the reasons (for selfishness).
Train consistently to deal with difficult
    situations.
Don't rely on other conditions.
Transform your attitude, but maintain your
    natural behavior.
Don't speak of others' faults,
Don't concern yourself with others' business.
Give up every hope of reward.
Avoid poisonous food.
Don't maintain misplaced loyalty.
Don't make malicious banter.
Don't lie in ambush.
Don't strike at the heart.
Don't place the load of a horse on a pony.
Don't sprint to win the race.
Don't turn gods into devils.
Don't seek others' misery as a means to
    happiness.

7. The Precepts of Mind Training

Every yoga should be performed as one.
There are two activities to be done at the
    beginning and end.
Train first in the easier practices.
Whichever occurs be patient with both.
Guard both at the cost of your life.
Train in the three difficulties.
Transform everything into the
    Great Vehicle path.
Value an encompassing and far-reaching
    practice.
Seek for the three principal conditions.
Purify the coarser one first.
Practice that which is more effective.
Don't let three factors weaken.
Never be parted from the three possessions.
If you relapse, meditate on it as the antidote.
Engage in the principal practices right now.
In the future, always put on armor.
Don't apply a wrong understanding.
Don't be sporadic.
Practice unflinchingly.
Be liberated by examination and analysis.
Don't be boastful.

Don't be short-tempered.
Don't make a short-lived attempt.
Don't expect gratitude.

What It Means to Practice

The phrase "practicing a religious system" is not given to mere physical change or living in a monastery or recitation. Religious practice must be carried out in terms of one's own thought. If one knows how to bring the teachings into one's own thought, all physical and verbal deeds can be made to accord with practice. If one does not know how to bring them into one's own thought, even though one might meditate, recite scriptures, or spend one's life in a temple, it will not help; thought, therefore, is important for practice. Thus, taking refuge in the Three Jewels (the Buddha, his Doctrine, and the Spiritual Community), taking into account the relationship between actions and their effects, and generating an attitude of helping others are most important.

Formerly in Tibet, there was a famous lama called Drom. One day Drom saw a man walking around a reliquary. "Walking around a reliquary is good," he said. "Practice is even better."

The man thought, *Then reading a holy book would be good.* He did so, and one day while he was reading, Drom saw him and said, "Reading a holy book is good; practice is even better."

The man thought, *This also does not seem to be sufficient. Now if I do some meditation, that will certainly be practice.*

Drom saw him in meditation and said, "Meditation is good; practice is even better."

The man was amazed and asked, "How does one practice?"

Drom answered, "Do not be attached to this life; cause your mind to become the practices." Drom said this because practice depends on thought.

EIGHT VERSES FOR TRAINING THE MIND

Eight Verses for Training the Mind is a short piece written by the Buddhist master Geshe Lang-ri Tang-pa (1054–1123), who saw the practice of the mind in enlightenment and, in particular, the meditation of exchanging the self with others as most important in his life. These verses were first explained to me when I was a small boy in Lhasa, and I have recited them every day since then as part of my personal practice.

> With the determination to accomplish
> The highest welfare of all sentient beings,
> Who surpass even a wish-granting jewel,
> I will learn to hold them supremely dear.

Whenever I associate with others I will learn
To think of myself as the lowest amongst all
And respectfully hold others to be supreme
From the very depths of my heart.

In all actions I will learn to search into my mind
And as soon as a disturbing emotion arises,
Endangering myself and others,
I will firmly face and avert it.

I will learn to cherish ill-natured beings
And those oppressed by strong
misdeeds and sufferings,
As if I had found a precious
Treasure difficult to find.

When others out of envy treat me badly
With abuse, slander, and the like,
I will learn to take all loss
And offer the victory to them.

When the one whom I have
benefited with great hope
Hurts me very badly without reason,
I will learn to view that person
As an excellent spiritual guide.

In short, I will learn to offer to
everyone without exception
All help and happiness directly and indirectly,
And respectfully take upon myself
All harm and suffering of my mothers.

I will learn to keep all those practices
Undefiled by the stains of
the eight worldly concerns,
And by understanding all
phenomena as like illusions,
Be released from the bondage of attachment.

In the first seven of these eight verses on training the mind, what is discussed is the conventional
awakening of the mind, known as Conventional
Bodhicitta. In the final verse, there is a very brief ref-
erence to the alternative form of bodhicitta—that is,
the Ultimate Bodhicitta.

— The **first** of these eight verses says: *Those with
determination to accomplish the higher welfare of sentient beings, who excel even the wish-fulfilling-gem—may
I at all times hold them dear!* What is being spoken of
here is the relationship between the self and others.
What is the usual situation in this regard? In general,

one can say that one cherishes—of course, with high regard—one's own self; one's own concerns; and, therefore, the task of achieving one's own welfare by finding happiness and avoiding suffering. This burden is borne by oneself as the precious chief concern. At the same time, concern for others is generally discarded as being of little importance, or even insignificant.

This situation needs to be changed by undertaking the mental training that reverses this attitude of paying high regard to one's own welfare and thinking of other people's welfare as insignificant. What is to be done is to develop a high regard and great concern for the welfare of others, meanwhile looking on one's own welfare as relatively insignificant. So this is the objective. In order to accomplish it, one requires a sustained mental training involving a number of different methods.

— The **second** verse of the text says: *Whenever I associate with others, may I think of myself as the lowest among all, and of the others as supreme, thinking thus from the depth of my heart.* Now the content of this line is in contrast with our previous attitude of looking down upon others. Rather, we are now looking up to all sentient beings or thinking of them as our own brothers, while regarding oneself as inferior to them. We are now cherishing them and devoting our body, mind, and entire being to the welfare of others, dedicating our self to the welfare of all creatures, now viewed as supreme.

— The **third** verse says: *In all actions, may I search into my mind and, as soon as clashes or mental distortions arise, thus endangering myself and others, may I firmly face and avert them.* In seeking to cultivate this attitude of cherishing others from the position of one who regards himself as looking up to them, one finds that this attitude is incompatible with various mental distortions—that is, the mental distortions that hitherto prevented us from escaping from self-love, prevented us from escaping from a false conception of self.

In view of this incompatibility, the verse stresses that we must guard against such mental distortions. When they arise in the mind, one must keep guard on one's thoughts as if one were guarding a house. This is to be done with mindfulness and discriminating awareness. These two are like inner watchers of the mind, resembling internal police. If these are present in the mind, then external police are not necessary, for one will not engage in unwholesome, harmful actions. However, if these inner guards, these inner police of mindfulness and discriminating awareness, are missing, no matter how many police you have outside, they will not be able to handle it. For example, we can see from the case of terrorists how ineffective the police can be.

— The **fourth** verse says: *When I see beings of evil nature oppressed by violent distortions, may they be as dear to me as if I had found a precious treasure.* This verse refers especially to beings that are somehow extremely disgusting, such as man-eaters or very evil beings. On meeting such beings, although we may not have any desire to harm them, we may very well have a natural inclination to try to avoid them—to avert our eyes, to have no contact with them.

This attitude, however, should be dispelled. What is to be cultivated, whether they are present or absent, is an affectionate concern for such beings so that when we meet them, we do not feel: *Oh! Now I shall have to do something about them; here is a burden I must take on, or here is some action I must take.* Rather, on encountering such beings, one should feel as if one has found a precious jewel, a treasure, or something very glorious, and eagerly accept this opportunity to help them.

— The **fifth** verse says: *When others are angry or mistreat me with abuse, slander, and the like, may I suffer defeat and offer the victory to them.* Hence, it is important to cultivate this attitude of being of service, this wish to cherish others, but one should especially take as the very central point of the practice the cultivation of such an attitude toward beings who, for whatever reason, have a magician's desire to harm us, whether from anger or a desire to let us down, and whether they harm us physically or simply wish us ill. One should have a special regard for beings such as these, as though they were very precious. With such sentient beings, if their attitude of malice toward oneself leads to some sort of conflict, what must be done is to accept defeat or loss for oneself and allow them the victory. This is the essence of the preceding verse.

— The **sixth** verse says: *When one whom I have benefited treats me very badly, may I hold him as my supreme guru.* Among the vast number of sentient beings, there may be some for whom one has made special efforts to be of service or shown some special kindness, which would be regarded as a noble and proper type of action. It would be fitting for such a person to repay that kindness and show some concern for his benefactor. But it can happen that when we have shown kindness to someone, he responds in a very poor and undeserved way, in which case our natural response would be to feel upset and unjustly treated.

Now, what is to be done by a bodhisattva—that is, someone cultivating this attitude—is to regard the other person as his own spiritual guru, taking what has happened as a tremendous opportunity and specially valuing this person as someone to be cherished. This is because he has given us a chance to cultivate patience and tolerance. It is in this way the bodhisattva cultivates this type of mental attitude.

— Now, we move to the **seventh** verse, which says: *In short, may I directly and indirectly offer benefit or happiness to all my mothers: May I secretly take upon myself their woes and sufferings.* This is still referring to the conventional awakening mind. So, now, in order for this fine attitude of cherishing others more than oneself to be developed very strongly and for it to become fervent, it needs to arise from the roots of compassion. Compassion is what is felt by a mind that cannot bear the suffering of others and longs for them to be freed from it. Besides feeling very earnestly a compassionate concern for others, we must also develop an attitude of loving-kindness in which one looks upon others' happiness and well-being with a feeling of joy.

These two—compassion and loving-kindness—are the root from which springs the active cherishing of others more than oneself. Upon these has been built a practice called Tong-Len (gTong-Len, or giving and taking) expressed by the verse: "May I offer benefit and happiness to all my mothers and take secretly upon myself their woes and suffering."

To be able to actually transfer one's happiness to others and directly take their sufferings upon oneself is something only possible on a very, very few occasions; it occurs when oneself and another individual have a very special type of relationship based on karmic affinity streaming, perhaps, from a previous life. On such occasions, it may be possible to actually cause a transference of suffering from another to oneself, but normally this is not possible. Then, why does one train people to cultivate this attitude? Because it leads to attaining great strength of character, courage, and enthusiasm; and this improves one's own practice of cultivating an awakening mind.

— The **eighth** and last verse of the text says: *May all this remain undefiled by the stains of the eight* *worldly concerns. May I, by perceiving that all the dharmas or constituents of phenomena are illusive, become unattached and thus be relieved from the bondage of cyclic existence.* In this final verse, the core meaning relates to the cultivation of the ultimate awakening of the mind. Whereas the other verses serve to relate directly to the types of practice, this one relates directly to the awakening of the mind.

To cultivate this mind of cherishing others more than oneself can involve a great danger because we have long been subject to mental distortions, which may interfere with one's practice of Dharma. One may be polluted with a concern for the reputation that could be won from this practice, or one may secretly desire to receive presents from individuals for whom one has performed the practice. Also, the thought can arise: *Oh, I am a religious person; I am a practitioner of Dharma!* This may lead to a sense of pride, of superiority to other beings, and to looking down upon them.

All these kinds of mental distortions and types of attitude relating to them are very apt to affect us. Because of this danger in cultivating this awakening of the mind, one should be especially on guard against the so-called eight worldly concerns. These eight include concern for fame, praise, pleasure, and gain. One must free the mind completely from these in practicing the Dharma. Cultivating this type of mind must be pure in the sense of having no concern at all for oneself and an unmarred concern for others. This is extremely important.

❧♡❧

Chapter Nine

MEANINGFUL
LIVING AND DYING

Something that preoccupies us all is how to live and die peacefully. Death is a form of suffering; it is an experience we would rather avoid, yet it is something that will definitely befall each and every one of us. Nevertheless, it is possible to adopt a course of action so that we can face this unwelcome event without fear. One of the principal factors that will help us remain calm and undisturbed at the time of death is the way we have lived our lives. The more we have made our lives meaningful, the less we will have to regret at the time of death. The way we feel when we come to die is thus very much dependent on the way we have lived.

Embarking on a spiritual practice that is measured in lifetimes and eons gives you a different perspective on death. In the context of your existence through many successive lives, death is something like changing your clothes. When your clothes become old and worn-out, you change them for new ones. This affects your attitude toward death. It gives rise to a clearer realization that death is a part of life. Grosser levels of mind are dependent on our brains, so they continue to function only as long as the brain functions. As soon as the brain stops, these levels of mind automatically stop. The brain is a condition for the appearance of grosser levels of mind, but the substantial cause of the mind is the continuity of the subtle mind, which has no beginning.

When we are dying, other people can remind us to generate positive states of mind up to the point at which the gross level of consciousness dissolves. But once we have entered the state of subtle consciousness, only the force of our previous predispositions can help. At that point it is very difficult for anyone else to remind us about virtuous practice. Therefore, it is important to develop an awareness of death and to become familiar with ways to cope with the dissolution of the mind right from the time of our youth. We can do this by rehearsing it through visualization.

Then, instead of being afraid of death, we may feel a sense of excitement about it. We may feel that having made preparations for so many years, we should be able to meet the challenge of death effectively.

Overcoming Fear

Once you have an experience of the deeper subtle mind in meditation, you can actually control your death. Of course, that can be done only when you reach an advanced level of practice. In tantra there are advanced practices such as the transference of consciousness, but I believe that the most important practice at the time of death is the awakening mind. That is what is most powerful. Although in my own daily practice I meditate on the process of death in association with various tantric practices seven or eight times a day, I am still convinced that I will find it easiest to remember the awakening mind when I die. That is the mind I really feel close to.

Of course, by meditating on death, we also prepare ourselves for it so we no longer need to worry about it. Although I am still not ready to face my actual death, I sometimes wonder how I will cope when actually faced with it. I am determined that if

I live longer, I will be able to accomplish much more. My will to live is equal to my excitement about facing death.

Remembering death is a part of Buddhist practice. There are different aspects to this. One is to meditate constantly about death as a means of enhancing detachment from this life and its attractions. Another aspect is to rehearse the process of death, to familiarize yourself with the different levels of mind that are experienced as you die. When coarser levels of mind cease, the subtler mind comes to the fore. Meditating on the process of death is important in order to gain a deeper experience of the subtle mind.

Death means that this body has certain limits. When the body can no longer be sustained, we die and take on a new body. The basic being or self that is designated onto the combination of body and mind persists after death, although the particular body is no more. The subtle body remains. From that point of view, the being has no beginning or end; it will remain until Buddhahood.

Nevertheless, people are afraid of death. Unless you can guarantee your future due to your positive actions during this lifetime, there is every danger of being reborn in an unfavorable state of existence. In this lifetime, even if you lose your own country and become a refugee, you are still living in the human world. You can seek help and support. But after death you encounter entirely new circumstances. The ordinary experience we gain in this life is generally of no help after death.

If you have not made proper preparations, things could be unfortunate. The way to prepare is by training the mind. On one level, this means cultivating a sincere, compassionate motivation and performing positive actions, serving other sentient beings. At another level, it means controlling your mind, which is a more profound way of preparing for the future. Eventually you can become master of your mind, which is the main purpose of meditation.

People who do not have any belief in anything after death would do better to think of death as just a part of life. Sooner or later we all have to face it, and at least that will help us to think of death as something normal. Even if we deliberately avoid thinking about death, we cannot escape it.

Faced with such a problem, you have two alternatives. One is simply not to think about it, to put it out of your mind. At least your mind will remain calm. But this is not a reliable option because the problem remains, and sooner or later you will have to face it. The other alternative is to face the problem, to think about it penetratingly. I know soldiers who say that their force is greater before they fight than when they actually go into battle. If you think about death, your mind will become familiar with the idea. When it actually takes place, it will be less of a shock and you will be less upset. Therefore, I think it is useful to think and talk about death.

We need to make our lives meaningful. In the scriptures, the realms of existence are described as impermanent, like a cloud in the autumn sky. The birth and death of human beings can be understood by watching the comings and goings of participants in a drama. You see the actors first in one costume and then in another. Within a short period of time, they undergo many changes. Our existence is also like that. The ebbing away of a human life is compared to lightning in the sky and the fall of a boulder down a steep incline.

Water always runs downhill. It is impossible that it will ever run uphill. Almost without our noticing it, our lives run out. Those of us who accept the value of spiritual practice may think about our future lives, but in our hearts we focus principally on the purposes of this life. This is how we become confused and entrapped in the cycle of existence. We waste our lives. Right from the time of our birth we are approaching death. Yet we spend our lives mainly amassing food, clothing, and friends. At the time of death, we have to leave all of this behind. We have to travel to the next world alone, unaccompanied.

The only thing that will benefit us is if we have undertaken some spiritual practice and have left some positive imprints within our minds. If we are to stop wasting our lives and provoke ourselves to do spiritual practice, we have to meditate on impermanence and our own mortality—the fact that from the moment of our birth our bodies are naturally impermanent and subject to disintegration.

Death as Spiritual Practice

Engaging in spiritual practices is not meant to just benefit this life, but to bring peace and happiness in the lives after death. One thing that hampers our practice is our tendency to think that we will live for a long time. We are like someone who has decided to settle down in a certain place. Such a person naturally becomes involved in the affairs of the world, amassing wealth, constructing buildings, planting crops, and so forth. On the other hand, the person who is more concerned about his or her lives after death is like a person who wants to travel. A traveler makes preparations to meet every eventuality and successfully reach his or her destination. As a result of death meditation, a practitioner becomes less obsessed with the affairs of this life—name and fame, possessions, social status. While working to meet the needs of this life, someone who meditates on death finds the time to generate the energy that can bring about peace and joy in future lives.

Awareness of death can be developed through both formal and analytical meditation. You must first understand the certainty of death intellectually. It is not some obscure theoretical issue, but an obvious and observable fact. Our world is believed to be some five billion years old, and the human race has been in existence for the last 100,000 years. Over such a long period of time, is there even one human being who did not have to face death? Death is absolutely inevitable regardless of where you live, whether you hide deep in the ocean or fly up into the open sky.

It makes no difference who you are; you have to die. Stalin and Mao were two of the most powerful men of the 20th century. Nevertheless, they, too, had to die; and it appears that they faced death with fear and unhappiness. When they were alive, they ruled as dictators. They were surrounded by attendants and lackeys ready to do their bidding. They ruled ruthlessly, ready to destroy anything that challenged their authority. But when they were faced with death, everyone they had trusted up to that point, everything they had relied on—their power, their weapons, their military force—was no longer of any use. Under such circumstances, anyone would feel afraid.

The advantage of developing an awareness of death is that it will help you make your life meaningful. You will regard the enduring peace and happiness as more important than short-term pleasure. Recollecting death is like using a hammer to destroy all negative tendencies and disturbing emotions.

In developing awareness of death, you need next to think about how unpredictable it is. This is expressed by a popular saying: "Tomorrow or the next life, you never know which will come first." We all know death will come one day. The problem is that we always think it will be sometime in the future. We are always busy with our worldly affairs. Therefore, it is essential to meditate on death's unpredictability. Traditional texts explain that the life span of the people of this world is uncertain, particularly in this degenerate age. Death does not follow any rule or order. Anyone can die at any time, whether they are old or young, rich or poor, sickly or well. Nothing can be taken for granted in relation to death. Strong, healthy people die suddenly due to unforeseen circumstances; while weak, bedridden patients hang on for a long time.

Comparing the causes that can lead to death with the limited factors that help sustain life, we can see why death is unpredictable. We hold this human body dear, believing that it is strong and will last a long time. But reality defies our hopes. Compared with rock and steel, our bodies are feeble and delicate. We eat to maintain our health and sustain our lives, but there are occasions when even food makes us sick and leads to our death. Nothing can guarantee that we will live forever.

Death is dreaded as the end of life. To make matters worse, nothing that we work for in this life—wealth, power, fame, friends, or family—can help at that time.

You may be a powerful person backed by a huge military force, but when death strikes, it cannot defend you. You may be wealthy and able to buy the best care when you are sick, but when death finally prevails, there is no expert you can hire who can forestall death. When you have to leave the world, your wealth stays behind. You cannot take a single penny with you. Your dearest friend cannot accompany you. You have to face the next world alone. Only your experience of spiritual practice can help you.

Your own body is very precious to you. It has been your most reliable, firmest companion since your very conception. You have done all you can to give it the best care. You have fed it so that it will not be hungry; you have given it drink when it was thirsty. You have rested when it was tired. You have been prepared to do anything and everything for the care, comfort, and protection of your body. In fairness, your body has also served you. It has always been ready to fulfill your needs. Just the function of the heart is a source of amazement. It is constantly at work. It literally never stops, whatever you do, whether you are asleep or awake.

But when death strikes, your body gives up. Your consciousness and your body separate, and your precious body becomes simply a dreadful corpse. Thus, in the face of death, your wealth and possessions, friends and relatives, and even your own body can do you no good. The only thing that can help you face the unknown is the virtue you have planted on the stream of your consciousness. This is why spiritual practice can help you make your life meaningful.

Remembering the awakening mind automatically brings calmness and peace of mind at the time of death. Cultivating a virtuous state of mind as you die can cause virtuous action to ripen and ensure a good rebirth. Therefore, from the point of view of a Buddhist practitioner, living a meaningful daily life means making yourself familiar with virtuous states of mind, which will eventually help you face death. Whether your experience at the time of death is positive or negative is very much dependent on how you have practiced during your life.

The important thing is that our day-to-day life should be meaningful . . . that our attitude should be positive, happy, and warm.

❧❧❧

Chapter Ten

UNDERSTANDING
EMPTINESS

The knowledge of external phenomena, and the application of that knowledge, is what we call science nowadays. The approach and methods that focus primarily on internal phenomena, and the application of internal phenomena, like consciousness or the mind, constitute another sphere of knowledge. Both have the same objective: the achievement of happiness and satisfaction, which are the intimate concerns of every human being.

Not only the objective, but the method, is also directly related to human beings, as it is the individual who puts it into action. The scientist investigating external phenomena is still a living human being who wants happiness; whether it is his profession or not, consciousness is also his concern. The spiritual person whose interest lies in consciousness or meditation has to deal with matter. No one single way is sufficient. Indeed, if just one approach had been found to be so, the need would never have been felt to bring these disciplines together.

Both approaches are therefore very important, and I would like to say a few words to relate them to one another.

Dependent Arising

The fundamental view or philosophy of Buddhism is that of "dependent arising." When one talks about the view of dependent arising, one means that things exist in dependence or that they are imputed depending on something or other. In the case of a physical phenomenon, one would specify that it exists in dependence on its parts, whereas non-physical composite phenomena would be described as existing in dependence either on their continuity or an aspect of their continuity. Consequently, whether it is external or internal phenomena, there is not anything that exists except in dependence upon its parts or aspects.

If one were to investigate a basis for the imputation in any given phenomenon, since one would not find any "thing" at all that actually *is* the phenomenon —no solid lump of anything that one could point one's finger at, which represents the phenomenon— then one says that phenomena exist through the imputation of the mind.

As phenomena do not exist independently of the imputing mind, one speaks of "emptiness," which means the lack of any intrinsic existence that does not depend upon the imputing mind. Since things do not exist just of their own accord, but in dependence on conditions, they change whenever they encounter different conditions. Thus, they come into existence in dependence on conditions, and they cease in dependence on conditions. That very lack of any intrinsic existence, independent of cause and conditions, is the basis for all the changes that are possible in a phenomenon, such as birth, cessation, and so forth.

It may be interesting to compare the scientific interpretation of the role of the observer or "participator" with the Buddhist view that observed phenomena do not exist merely as a mental image, a projection, or vision of the mind, but rather that they exist as separate entities from the mind. Mind and matter are two separate things. Matter is separate from the mind that cognizes it and denominates it.

This means that with regard to all phenomena without exception, although they are not simply a creation or manifestation of the mind having no entity of their own, their ultimate mode of existence is dependent on the mind that imputes them as the "imputer." Their mode of existence is therefore quite separate from the imputer, but their existence itself is dependent on the imputer. I feel that this point of view perhaps corresponds to the scientific explanation of the role of the observer. Although different terms are employed to explain them, their meanings are somewhat related.

The Real Nature of Phenomena

On the surface, the dependent arising and emptiness explained above may seem to be quite contradictory. Yet if one analyzes them on a much deeper level, one can come to understand that phenomena, on account of their being empty, are dependently arising or dependently existing, and because of that dependent existence, they are empty by nature. Thus, one can establish both emptiness and dependent arising on one single basis, and thereby two faces that on a general level seem to be contradictory, when understood on a profound level will be seen to fit together in a complementary fashion.

The mode of appearance of phenomena is differentiated from their actual mode of existence. When the mind apprehends their way of appearing, believes in that appearance as being true, and follows that particular idea or concept, then one makes mistakes. Since that concept is completely distorted in its apprehension of the object, it contradicts the actual mode of existence, or reality itself. So, this disparity or contradiction between "what is" and "what appears" is due to the fact that although phenomena are in reality empty of any intrinsic nature, they do appear to the ordinary mind as if they exist inherently, even though they lack any such quality. Similarly, although in reality things that depend on causes are impermanent and transient, undergoing constant change, they do *appear* as though they were permanent and unchanging.

Again, something that in its true nature is suffering appears as happiness. And something that is in reality false appears as true. There are many levels of subtlety regarding this contradiction between the mode of existence of phenomena and their mode of appearance. As a result of the contradiction between "what is" and "what appears," there arise all manner of mistakes. This explanation may have much in common with scientists' views of the difference in the modes of appearance and existence of certain phenomena.

Generally speaking, an understanding of the meaning of emptiness and dependent arising will naturally lead one to a deeper conviction in the law of cause and effect, where as a result of different causes and conditions, corresponding fruits or effects, positive or negative, arise. One will then pay more attention to the causes and also be more aware of the various conditions. If one has a good understanding of emptiness or familiarity with it, then the arising of distortions, like attachment, hatred, and so on, in the mind will diminish, since they are caused by a mistaken view—mistaken in not correctly distinguishing between "what is" and "what appears."

You can see, for instance, from your own experience, how your feeling toward something that you observe will change, depending on your own state of mind. Although the object remains the same, your reaction will be far less intense when your mind is calm than if it is overcome by some strong emotional feeling like anger.

The actual mode of existence of phenomena, the bare thought of existence, is emptiness. When one understands this and appreciates the contradictory nature of the appearance of phenomena, one will immediately be able to realize this mistaken view to be untrue. Consequently, all mental distortions such as attachment, hatred, and the like—which are based on that misconception, a deception rooted in the contradictory nature of phenomena—will decrease in strength.

We might ask: *How do the different levels of consciousness or mind that apprehend an object actually come to exist themselves?* Different levels of consciousness are in relation to the different levels of subtlety of the inner energy that activates and moves consciousness toward a given object. So, the level of subtlety and strength in moving consciousness toward the object determines and establishes the different levels of consciousness.

It is very important to reflect upon the relationship between the inner consciousness and outer material substances. Many Eastern philosophies, and in particular, Buddhism, speak of four elements: earth, water, fire, and air . . . or five elements with the addition of space. The first four elements—earth, water, fire, and air—are supported by the element of space, which enables them to exist and to function. Space or "ether" serves, then, as the basis for the functioning of all the elements.

These five elements can be divided into two types: the outer five elements and the inner five elements, and there is a definite relationship between the outer and inner elements. The element space or "ether," according to certain Buddhist texts, such as the Kalachakra Tantra, is not just a total voidness, devoid of anything, but it is referred to in terms of "empty particles." This empty particle therefore serves as the basis for the evolution and dissolution of the four other elements. They are generated from it and finally are absorbed back into it. The process of dissolution evolves in the order *earth, water, fire,* and *air;* and the process of generation in the order *air, fire, water,* and *earth.* These four are better understood in terms of: solidity (earth), liquids (water), heat (fire), and energy (air). The four elements are generated from the subtle level to the gross, out of this basis of empty particles; and they dissolve from the gross level to the subtle into the empty particles. Space, or the empty particle, is the basis for the whole process.

Meditation on Emptiness

To realize that all deceptive phenomena are the same in their nature of emptiness, we concentrate on emptiness. When meditation on the mind of enlightenment and also training in concentration has matured, then the practice of emptiness begins.

Generally it is not necessary to withdraw the appearance of the object when we meditate on emptiness, but as we are concerned here with tantric practices, the appearance of the objects is recommended to be withdrawn.

We can start this practice in either of two ways: We can first dissolve all appearances and then meditate on emptiness, or first meditate on emptiness and then dissolve all appearances of the objects.

Now to explain briefly the actual meditation on emptiness. . . . Here, it is very important to identify what is to be negated.

The major Buddhist schools accept what are known as the four Buddhist seals. These four are as follows:

- All products are impermanent.

- All contaminated phenomena are in the nature of suffering.

- All phenomena are selfless and empty.

- Nirvana alone is peace.

Here, selflessness refers to the emptiness of a self-sufficient person.

First, in order to meditate on emptiness, we have to identify the emptiness upon which we are meditating—the thing to be negated. Unless we identify the object of negation, we cannot have the image of its absence. For this it is more convenient first to reflect on one's own self.

When you have this natural feeling of "I do, I eat, I stay," just contemplate what kind of self or "I" appears to your mind. Then try different techniques. Try to recollect unpleasant situations in which, for example, you were unjustly blamed for something, or pleasant situations in which you were praised. During such experiences, you had a very fluctuating state of mind, and at that time it seemed you could sense that "I," that self, quite clearly.

When this "I" appeared to your mind, did it appear as something separate from your body and mind, like an independent entity? That type of "I" or self, which appears to you so vividly that you feel you could put your finger on it—something independent from your own body and mind—that type of "I" is the most misconceived projection, and that is the object of negation.

This is the first essential part: identifying what is to be negated.

The second essential point is to reflect on whether if such an "I" or independent self exists, it does so as one with the body and mind or truly separate from them, or if there is a third way in which it can exist.

You have to look at the different possibilities, and then you will find that if it truly exists as an independent entity, it should be either one with the body and mind, the aggregates, or it should be separate, because there is no third way of existence.

That is the second essential point: The choices are that it is either one with the aggregates or totally different from them.

Now reflect on the idea that if it is one with the aggregates, then just as the self is one, body and mind should be one because they are identified with the self. If the self is separate, then just as the aggregates are manifold, in the same way the self should be manifold.

Then contemplate that if this independent self or "I" existed as something distinctly separate, truly apart from the aggregates, then it should be findable even after the aggregates ceased to exist. But this is not the case.

When you search by this mode of inquiry, you will find that such an "I" cannot be identified from the side of the aggregates.

Reasoning thus, you will find that the independent "I" or self that previously appeared to your consciousness is a misconception or projection. It does not exist.

For example, at dawn or dusk, when there is not much light, someone might get frightened and might mistake a coiled rope for a snake. Apart from the image of the snake in the mind of that person, there is no sense of true existence of a snake on the part of the object, the rope.

It is the same with the aggregates. When you perceive the appearances of the self in them, although such appearances seem to arise from within the aggregates, there is not the slightest particle that can be identified as the self within the aggregates. Just as in the earlier example wherein the snake is only a misconceived projection—there is no true existence of the snake.

In the same way, when we have the appearance or apprehension of a person as distinct from the aggregates, from the side of the aggregates there is no true existence of the person; there is only a label imputed on the aggregates. As long as there is no essence existing on the part of the object concerned, in both cases they are the same.

As far as the states of the object from the side of the object are concerned, there is no difference at all between them. The difference has to come from the perceiving mind, from the side of the subject. When we label that coiled rope as a snake, that is a mistaken conception. After a while the sun rises; we get a clear view of the object and can dispel the misconception of that rope as a snake by valid cognition, a different type of consciousness.

That label of *snake* on the coiled rope can be harmful. However, in the case of a person, although there is no objective reality, if you label the aggregates as the person, it serves the purpose. There is no other type of consciousness that can dispel that.

However, if we were to say that therefore there is no person at all, then our own experiences would contradict our false conclusion. Hence, the existence of the person has to be justified only from the subjective consciousness that gives the label. For this reason, things are said to exist only nominally. There is no objective reality.

Chapter Eleven

UNIVERSAL RESPONSIBILITY

I should mention that I do not believe in creating movements or espousing ideologies. Nor do I like the practice of establishing an organization to promote a particular idea, which implies that one group of people alone is responsible for the attainment of that goal, while everybody else is exempt. In our present circumstances, none of us can afford to assume that somebody else will solve our problems; each of us must take his or her own share of universal responsibility. In this way, as the number of concerned, responsible individuals grows, tens, hundreds, thousands, or even hundreds of thousands of such people will greatly improve the general atmosphere. Positive change does not come quickly and demands ongoing effort. If we become discouraged, we may not attain even the simplest goals. With constant, determined application, we can accomplish even the most difficult objectives.

Adopting an attitude of universal responsibility is essentially a personal matter. The real test of compassion is not what we say in abstract discussions, but how we conduct ourselves in daily life. Still, certain fundamental views are basic to the practice of altruism. Although no system of government is perfect, democracy is closest to humanity's essential nature. Hence, those of us who enjoy it must continue to fight for all people's right to do so. Furthermore, democracy is the only stable foundation upon which a global political structure can be built. To work as one, we must respect the right of all peoples and nations to maintain their own distinctive character and values.

In particular, a tremendous effort will be required to bring compassion into the realm of international business. Economic inequality, especially that between developed and developing nations, remains the greatest source of suffering on this planet.

Even though they will lose money in the short term, large multinational corporations must curtail their exploitation of poor nations. Tapping the few precious resources such countries possess simply to fuel consumerism in the developed world is disastrous; if it continues unchecked, eventually we shall all suffer. Strengthening weak, undiversified economies is a far wiser policy for promoting both political and economic stability. As idealistic as it may sound, altruism, not just competition and the desire for wealth, should be a driving force in business.

We also need to renew our commitment to human values in the field of modern science. Although the main purpose of science is to learn more about reality, another of its goals is to improve the quality of life. Without altruistic motivation, scientists cannot distinguish between beneficial technologies and the merely expedient. The environmental damage surrounding us is the most obvious example of the result of this confusion, but proper motivation may be even more relevant in governing how we handle the extraordinary new array of biological techniques with which we can now manipulate the subtle structures of life itself. If we do not base our every action on an ethical foundation, we run the risk of inflicting terrible harm on the delicate matrix of life.

Nor are the religions of the world exempt from this responsibility. The purpose of religion is not to build beautiful churches or temples, but to cultivate positive human qualities such as tolerance, generosity, and love. Every world religion, no matter what its philosophical view, is founded first and foremost on the precept that we must reduce our selfishness and serve others. Unfortunately, sometimes religion itself causes more quarrels than it solves. Practitioners of different faiths should realize that each religious tradition has immense intrinsic value and the means for providing mental and spiritual health.

One religion, like a single type of food, cannot satisfy everybody. According to their varying mental dispositions, some people benefit from one kind of teaching, others from another. Each faith has the ability to produce fine, warmhearted people; and despite their espousal of often-contradictory philosophies, all religions have succeeded in doing so. Thus, there is no reason to engage in divisive religious bigotry and intolerance, and every reason to cherish and respect all forms of spiritual practice.

We are in the most painful period in human history—a time when, because of the vast increase in the destructive power of weapons, more people have suffered from and died by violence than ever before. Furthermore, we have also witnessed an almost terminal competition between the fundamental ideologies that have always torn the human community: force and raw power on the one hand; and freedom, pluralism, individual rights, and democracy on the other.

I believe that the results of this great competition are now clear. Although the good human spirit of peace, freedom, and democracy still faces many forms of tyranny and evil, it is nevertheless an unmistakable fact that the vast majority of people everywhere want it to triumph. Thus, the tragedies of our time have not been entirely without benefit and have in many cases been the very means by which the human mind has been opened. The collapse of Communism demonstrates this.

Although Communism espoused many noble ideals, including altruism, the attempt by its governing elites to dictate their views has proved disastrous. These governments went to tremendous lengths to control the entire flow of information through their societies and to structure their education systems so that their citizens would work for the common good. Although rigid organization may have been necessary in the beginning to destroy previously oppressive regimes, once that goal was fulfilled, the organization had very little to contribute toward building a useful human community. Communism failed utterly because it relied on force to promote its beliefs. Ultimately, human nature was unable to sustain the suffering it produced.

Brute force, no matter how strongly applied, can never subdue the basic human desire for freedom. The hundreds of thousands of people who marched in the cities of Eastern Europe proved this. They simply expressed the human need for freedom and democracy. It was very moving. Their demands had nothing whatsoever to do with some new ideology; these people simply spoke from their hearts, sharing their desire for freedom, demonstrating that it stems from the core of human nature.

Freedom, in fact, is the very source of creativity for both individuals and society. It is not enough, as Communist systems have assumed, merely to provide people with food, shelter, and clothing. If we have all these things but lack the precious air of liberty to sustain our deeper nature, we are only half human; we are like animals who are content just to satisfy their physical needs.

I feel that the peaceful revolutions in the former Soviet Union and Eastern Europe have taught us many great lessons. One is the value of truth. People do not like to be bullied, cheated, or lied to by either an individual or a system. Such acts are contrary to the essential human spirit. Therefore, even though those who practice deception and use force may achieve considerable short-term success, eventually they will be overthrown.

On the other hand, everyone appreciates truth, and respect for it is really in our blood. Truth is the best guarantor and the real foundation of freedom and democracy. It does not matter whether you are weak or strong or whether your cause has many or few adherents; truth will still prevail. The fact that the successful freedom movements of 1989 and after have been based on the true expression of people's most basic feelings is a valuable reminder that truth itself is still seriously lacking in much of our political life.

Especially in the conduct of international relations, we pay very little respect to truth. Inevitably, weaker nations are manipulated and oppressed by stronger ones, just as the weaker sections of most societies suffer at the hands of the more affluent and powerful. Although in the past, the simple expression of truth has usually been dismissed as unrealistic, these last few years have proven that it is an immense force in the human mind and, as a result, in the shaping of history.

A second great lesson from Eastern Europe has been that of peaceful change. In the past, enslaved peoples often resorted to violence in their struggle to be free. Now, following in the footsteps of Mahatma Gandhi and Martin Luther King, Jr., these peaceful revolutions offer future generations a wonderful example of successful, nonviolent change. When in the future major changes in society again become necessary, our descendants will be able to look back on the present time as a paradigm of peaceful struggle —a real success story of unprecedented scale, involving more than a dozen nations and hundreds of millions of people. Moreover, recent events have shown that the desire for both peace and freedom lies at the most fundamental level of human nature, and that violence is its complete antithesis.

I think it is vital to address the question of violence, whose elimination at every level is the necessary foundation for world peace and the ultimate goal of any international order.

Every day the media reports incidents of terrorism, crime, and aggression. I have never been to a country where tragic stories of death and bloodshed have not filled the newspapers and airwaves. Such reporting has become almost an addiction for journalists and their audiences alike. But the overwhelming majority of the human race does not behave destructively; very few of the five billion people on this planet actually commit acts of violence. Most of us prefer to be as peaceful as possible.

Basically, we all cherish tranquility, even those of us given to violence. For instance, when spring comes, the days grow longer, there is more sunshine, the grass and trees come alive, and everything is very fresh. People feel happy. In autumn, one leaf falls, then another; then all the beautiful flowers die until we are surrounded by bare, naked plants. We do not feel so joyful. Why is this? Because deep down, we desire constructive, fruitful growth and dislike things collapsing, dying, or being destroyed. Every destructive action goes against our basic nature; building, being constructive, is the human way.

I am sure everybody agrees that we need to overcome violence, but if we are to eliminate it completely, we should first analyze whether or not it has any value. If we address this question from a strictly practical perspective, we find that on certain occasions violence indeed appears useful. One can solve a problem quickly with force. At the same time, however, such success is often at the expense of the rights and welfare of others. As a result, even though one problem has been solved, the seed of another has been planted.

On the other hand, if one's cause is supported by sound reasoning, there is no point in using violence. It is those who have no motive other than selfish desire and who cannot achieve their goal through logical reasoning who rely on force. Even when family and friends disagree, those with valid reasons can cite them one after the other and argue their case point by point, whereas those with little rational support soon fall prey to anger. Thus, anger is not a sign of strength but one of weakness. Ultimately, it is important to examine one's own motivation and that of one's opponent.

There are many kinds of violence and nonviolence, but one cannot distinguish them by external factors alone. If one's motivation is negative, the action it produces is, in the deepest sense, violent, even though it may appear to be smooth and gentle. Conversely, if one's motivation is sincere and positive but the circumstances require harsh behavior, essentially one is practicing nonviolence. No matter what the case may be, I feel that compassionate concern for the benefit of others—not simply for oneself—is the sole justification for the use of force.

The genuine practice of nonviolence is still somewhat experimental on our planet, but its pursuit, based on love and understanding, is sacred. If this experiment succeeds, it can open the way to a far more peaceful world.

I have heard the occasional Westerner maintain that long-term Gandhian struggles employing nonviolent passive resistance do not suit everybody, and that such courses of action are more natural in the East. Because Westerners are active, they tend to seek immediate results in all situations, even at the cost of their lives. This approach, I believe, is not always beneficial. But surely the practice of nonviolence suits us all. It simply calls for determination. Even though the freedom movements of Eastern Europe reached their goals quickly, nonviolent protest by its very nature usually requires patience.

In this regard, I pray that despite the brutality of their suppression and the difficulty of the struggle they face, those involved in China's democratic movement will always remain peaceful. I am confident they will. Although the majority of the young Chinese students involved were born and raised under an especially harsh form of Communism, during the spring of 1989 they spontaneously practiced Mahatma Gandhi's strategy of passive resistance. This is remarkable and clearly shows that ultimately all human beings want to pursue the path of peace, no matter how much they have been indoctrinated.

✦

I see Tibet as what I have previously called a "zone of peace": a neutral, demilitarized sanctuary where weapons are forbidden and the people live in harmony with nature. This is not merely a dream—it is precisely the way Tibetans tried to live for over a thousand years before our country was invaded. As everybody knows, in Tibet all forms of wildlife were strictly protected in accordance with Buddhist principles. Also, for at least the last 300 years, we had no proper army. Tibet gave up the waging of war as an instrument of national policy in the 6th and 7th centuries, after the reign of our three great religious kings.

On the subject of developing regional communities and the task of disarmament, I would like to suggest that the "heart" of each community could be one or more nations that have decided to become zones of peace, areas from which military forces are prohibited. This, again, is not just a dream. In December 1948, Costa Rica disbanded its army. In 1989, 37 percent of the Swiss population voted to disband its military. If its people so choose, a nation can take radical steps to change its very nature.

Zones of peace within regional communities would serve as oases of stability. While paying their fair share of the costs of any collective force created by the community as a whole, these zones of peace would be the forerunners and beacons of an entirely peaceful world and would be exempt from engaging in any conflict. If regional communities do develop in Asia, South America, and Africa, and disarmament progresses so that an international force from all regions is created, these zones of peace will be able to expand, spreading tranquility as they grow.

I have not included the United Nations in this discussion of the present era because both its critical role in helping create a better world and its great potential for doing so are so well known. By definition, the United Nations must be in the very middle of whatever major changes occur. However, it may need to amend its structure for the future. I have always had the greatest hopes for the United Nations, and with no criticism intended, I would like simply to point out that the post–World War II climate under which its charter was conceived has changed. With that change has come the opportunity to further democratize the U.N., especially the somewhat exclusive Security Council, with its five permanent members, which should be made more representative.

I feel optimistic about the future. Some recent trends portend our great potential for a better world.

As late as the '50s and '60s, people believed that war was an inevitable condition of mankind. The Cold War, in particular, reinforced the notion that opposing political systems could only clash, not compete or even collaborate. Few now hold this view. Today, people all over the planet are genuinely concerned about world peace. They are far less interested in propounding ideology and far more committed to coexistence. These are very positive developments.

Also, for thousands of years people believed that only an authoritarian organization employing rigid disciplinary methods could govern human society. However, people have an innate desire for freedom and democracy, and these two forces have been in conflict. Today, it is clear which has won. The emergence of nonviolent "people's power" movements has shown indisputably that the human race can neither tolerate nor function properly under the rule of tyranny. This recognition represents remarkable progress.

Another hopeful development is the growing compatibility between science and religion. Throughout the 19th century and for much of the 20th, people have been profoundly confused by the conflict between these apparently contradictory worldviews. Today, physics, biology, and psychology have reached such sophisticated levels that many researchers are starting to ask the most profound questions about the ultimate nature of the universe and life, the same questions that are of prime interest to religions.

Thus, there is real potential for a more unified view. In particular, it seems that a new concept of mind and matter is emerging. The East has been more concerned with understanding the mind, the West with understanding matter. Now that the two have met, these spiritual and material views of life may become more harmonized.

The rapid changes in our attitude toward the earth are also a source of hope. As recently as 10 or 15 years ago, we thoughtlessly consumed its resources, as if there was no end to them. Now, not only individuals, but governments as well, are seeking a new ecological order. I often joke that the moon and stars look beautiful, but if any of us tried to live on them, we would be miserable. This blue planet of ours is the most delightful habitat we know. Its life is our life; its future, our future. And although I do not believe that the earth itself is a sentient being, it does indeed act as our mother; and, like children, we are dependent upon her.

Now Mother Nature is telling us to cooperate. In the face of such global problems as the greenhouse effect and the deterioration of the ozone layer, individual organizations and single nations are help-less. Unless we all work together, no solution will be found. Our mother is teaching us a lesson in universal responsibility.

I think we can say that, because of the lessons we have begun to learn, this century will be friendlier, more harmonious, and less harmful. Compassion, the seed of peace, will be able to flourish. I am very hopeful. At the same time, I believe that every individual has a responsibility to help guide our global family in the right direction. Good wishes alone are not enough; we have to assume responsibility. Large human movements spring from individual human initiatives. If you feel that you cannot have much of an effect, the next person may also become discouraged, and a great opportunity will have been lost. On the other hand, each of us can inspire others simply by working to develop our own altruistic motivation.

I am sure that many honest, sincere people all over the world already hold the views that I have mentioned here. Unfortunately, nobody listens to them. Although my voice may go unheeded as well, I thought that I should try to speak on their behalf. Of course, some people may feel that it is very presumptuous for the Dalai Lama to write in this way.

But, since I received the Nobel Peace Prize, I feel I have a responsibility to do so. If I just took the Nobel money and spent it however I liked, it would look as if the only reason I had spoken all those nice words in the past was to get this prize! However, now that I have received it, I must repay the honor by continuing to advocate the views that I have always expressed.

I, for one, truly believe that individuals can make a difference in society. Since periods of great change such as the present one come so rarely in human history, it is up to each of us to make the best use of our time to help create a happier world.

❧❦❧

Chapter Twelve

SCIENCE AT THE CROSSROADS

This chapter is based on a talk given by the Dalai Lama at the annual meeting of the Society for Neuroscience on November 12, 2005, in Washington, D.C.

The last few decades have witnessed tremendous advances in the scientific understanding of the human brain, and the human body as a whole. Furthermore, with new developments in genetics, neuroscience's knowledge of the workings of biological organisms is now brought to the subtlest level of individual genes. This has resulted in unforeseen technological possibilities of even manipulating the very codes of life, thereby giving rise to the likelihood of creating entirely new realities for humanity as a whole.

Today the question of science's interface with wider humanity is no longer a matter of academic interest alone; this question must assume a sense of urgency for all those who are concerned about the fate of human existence. I feel, therefore, that a dialogue between neuroscience and society could have profound benefits in that it may help deepen our basic understanding of what it means to be human and our responsibilities for the natural world we share with other sentient beings. I am glad to note that as part of this wider interface, there is a growing interest among some neuroscientists in engaging in deeper conversations with Buddhist contemplative disciplines.

Although my own interest in science began as the curiosity of a restless young boy growing up in Tibet, gradually the colossal importance of science and technology for understanding the modern world dawned on me. Not only have I sought to grasp specific scientific ideas, but I have also attempted to explore the wider implications of the new advances in human knowledge and technological power brought about through science. The specific areas of science I have explored most over the years are subatomic physics, cosmology, biology, and psychology. For my limited understanding of these fields I am deeply indebted to the hours of generous time shared with me by Carl von Weizsäcker and the late David Bohm, both of whom I consider to be my teachers in quantum mechanics; and in the field of biology, especially neuroscience, by the late Robert Livingston and Francisco Varela. I am also grateful to the numerous eminent scientists with whom I have had the privilege of engaging in conversations through the auspices of the Mind and Life Institute, which initiated the Mind and Life conferences that began in 1987 at my residence in Dharamsala, India. These dialogues have continued over the years and, in fact, the latest Mind and Life dialogue concluded here in Washington recently.

Some might wonder: *What is a Buddhist monk doing taking such a deep interest in science? What relation could there be between Buddhism, an ancient Indian philosophical and spiritual tradition, and modern science? What possible benefit could there be for a scientific discipline such as neuroscience in engaging in dialogue with the Buddhist contemplative tradition?*

Although the Buddhist contemplative tradition and modern science have evolved from different historical, intellectual, and cultural roots, I believe that at heart they share significant commonalities, especially in their basic philosophical outlook and methodology.

On the philosophical level, both Buddhism and modern science share a deep suspicion of any notion of absolutes, whether conceptualized as a transcendent being; as an eternal, unchanging principle such as soul; or as a fundamental substratum of reality. Both Buddhism and science prefer to account for the evolution and emergence of the cosmos and life in terms of the complex interrelations of the natural laws of cause and effect.

From the methodological perspective, both traditions emphasize the role of empiricism. For example, in the Buddhist investigative tradition, between the three recognized sources of knowledge—experience, reason, and testimony—it is the evidence of experience that takes precedence, with reason coming second and testimony last. This means that in the Buddhist investigation of reality, at least in principle, empirical evidence should triumph over scriptural authority, no matter how deeply venerated a scripture may be. Even in the case of knowledge derived through reason or inference, its validity must derive ultimately from some observed facts of experience. Because of this methodological standpoint, I have often remarked to my Buddhist colleagues that the empirically verified insights of modern cosmology and astronomy must compel us now to modify, or in some cases reject, many aspects of traditional cosmology as found in ancient Buddhist texts.

Since the primary motive underlying the Buddhist investigation of reality is the fundamental quest for overcoming suffering and perfecting the human condition, the primary orientation of the Buddhist investigative tradition has been toward understanding the human mind and its various functions. The assumption here is that by gaining deeper insight into the human psyche, we might find ways of transforming our thoughts, emotions, and their underlying propensities so that a more wholesome and fulfilling way of being can be found. It is in this context that the Buddhist tradition has devised a rich classification of mental states, as well as contemplative techniques for refining specific mental qualities.

So, a genuine exchange between the cumulative knowledge and experience of Buddhism and modern science on wide-ranging issues pertaining to the human mind, from cognition and emotion to understanding the capacity for transformation inherent in the human brain, can be deeply interesting and potentially beneficial as well. In my own experience,

I have felt deeply enriched by engaging in conversations with neuroscientists and psychologists on such questions as the nature and role of positive and negative emotions, attention, and imagery, as well as the plasticity of the brain. The compelling evidence from neuroscience and medical science of the crucial role of simple physical touch for even the physical enlargement of an infant's brain during the first few weeks powerfully brings home the intimate connection between compassion and human happiness.

Buddhism has long argued for the tremendous potential for transformation that exists naturally in the human mind. To this end, the tradition has developed a wide range of contemplative techniques, or meditation practices, aimed specifically at two principal objectives—the cultivation of a compassionate heart and the cultivation of deep insights into the nature of reality, which are referred to as the union of compassion and wisdom. At the heart of these meditation practices lie two key techniques: the refinement of attention and its sustained application on the one hand, and the regulation and transformation of emotions on the other. In both of these cases, I feel there might be great potential for collaborative research between the Buddhist contemplative tradition and neuroscience.

For example, modern neuroscience has developed a rich understanding of the brain mechanisms that are associated with both attention and emotion. The Buddhist contemplative tradition, given its long history of interest in the practice of mental training, offers, on the other hand, practical techniques for refining attention and regulating and transforming emotion. The meeting of modern neuroscience and the Buddhist contemplative discipline, therefore, could lead to the possibility of studying the impact of intentional mental activity on the brain circuits that have been identified as critical for specific mental processes.

At the very least such an interdisciplinary encounter could help raise critical questions in many key areas. For example, do individuals have a fixed capacity to regulate their emotions and attention; or, as the Buddhist tradition argues, is their capacity for regulating these processes greatly amenable to change, suggesting a similar degree of amenability of the behavioral and brain systems associated with these functions?

One area in which the Buddhist contemplative tradition may have an important contribution to make is the practical techniques it has developed for training in compassion. With regard to mental training both in attention and emotional regulation, it also becomes crucial to raise the question of whether any specific techniques have time-sensitivity in terms of their effectiveness so that new methods can be tailored to suit the needs of age, health, and other variable factors.

A note of caution is called for, however. It is inevitable that when two radically different investigative traditions like Buddhism and neuroscience are brought together in an interdisciplinary dialogue, this will involve problems that are normally attendant to exchanges across boundaries of cultures and disciplines.

For example, when we speak of the "science of meditation," we need to be sensitive to exactly what is meant by such a statement. On the part of scientists I feel it is important to be sensitive to the different connotations of an important term such as *meditation* in their traditional context. For example, in its traditional context, the term for meditation is *bhavana* (in Sanskrit) or *gom* (in Tibetan). The Sanskrit term connotes the idea of cultivation, such as cultivating a particular habit or a way of being, while the Tibetan term *gom* has the connotation of cultivating familiarity. So, briefly stated, meditation in the traditional Buddhist context refers to a deliberate mental activity that involves cultivating familiarity, be it with a chosen object, fact, theme, habit, outlook, or way of being.

Broadly speaking, there are two categories of meditation practice—one focusing on stilling the mind and the other on the cognitive processes of understanding. The two are referred to as (i) stabilizing meditation and (ii) discursive meditation. In both cases, the meditation can take many different forms.

For example, it may take the form of taking something as the object of one's cognition, such as meditating on one's transient nature. Or it may take the form of cultivating a specific mental state such as compassion by developing a heartfelt, altruistic yearning to alleviate others' suffering. Or it could take the form of imagination, exploring the human potential for generating mental imagery, which may be used in various ways to cultivate mental well-being.

So, it is critical to be aware of what specific forms of meditation one might be investigating when engaged in collaborative research so that the complexity of meditative practices being studied is matched by the sophistication of the scientific research.

Another area where a critical perspective is required on the part of the scientists is the ability to distinguish between the empirical aspects of Buddhist thought and contemplative practice, and the philosophical and metaphysical assumptions associated with these meditative practices. In other words, just as we must distinguish within the scientific approach between theoretical suppositions, empirical observations based on experiments, and subsequent interpretations, in the same manner it is critical to distinguish theoretical suppositions, experientially verifiable features of mental states, and subsequent philosophical interpretations in Buddhism. This way, both parties in the dialogue can find the common ground of empirical, observable facts of the human mind, while not falling into the temptation of reducing the framework of one discipline into that of the other.

Although the philosophical presuppositions and the subsequent conceptual interpretations may differ between these two investigative traditions . . . insofar as empirical facts are concerned, facts must remain facts, no matter how one may choose to describe them. Whatever the truth about the final nature of consciousness—whether or not it is ultimately reducible to physical processes—I believe there can be a shared understanding of the experiential facts of the various aspects of our perceptions, thoughts, and emotions.

With these precautionary considerations, I believe a close cooperation between these two investigative traditions can truly contribute toward expanding the human understanding of the complex world of inner subjective experience that we call the mind. Already the benefits of such collaborations are beginning to be demonstrated. According to preliminary reports, the effects of mental training—such as a simple mindfulness practice on a regular basis or the deliberate cultivation of compassion as developed in Buddhism—in bringing about observable changes in the human brain correlated to positive mental states can be measured.

Recent discoveries in neuroscience have demonstrated the innate plasticity of the brain—both in terms of synaptic connections and the birth of new neurons—as a result of exposure to external stimuli, such as voluntary physical exercise and an enriched environment. The Buddhist contemplative tradition may help to expand this field of scientific inquiry by proposing types of mental training that may also pertain to neuroplasticity. If it turns out, as the Buddhist tradition implies, that mental practice can effect observable synaptic and neural changes in the brain, this could have far-reaching implications.

The repercussions of such research will not be confined simply to expanding our knowledge of the human mind, but, perhaps more important, they could have great significance for our understanding of education and mental health. Similarly, if, as the Buddhist tradition claims, the deliberate cultivation of compassion can lead to a radical shift in the individual's outlook, leading to greater empathy toward others, this could have far-reaching implications for society at large.

Finally, I believe that the collaboration between neuroscience and the Buddhist contemplative tradition may shed fresh light on the vitally important question of the interface of ethics and neuroscience. Regardless of whatever conception one might have of the relationship between ethics and science, in actual practice science has evolved primarily as an empirical discipline with a morally neutral, value-free stance. It has come to be perceived essentially as a mode of inquiry that gives detailed knowledge of the empirical world and the underlying laws of nature.

Purely from the scientific point of view, the creation of nuclear weapons is a truly amazing achievement. However, since this creation has the potential to inflict so much suffering through unimaginable death and destruction, we regard it as destructive. It is the ethical evaluation that must determine what is positive and what is negative. Until recently, this approach of segregating ethics and science, with the understanding that the human capacity for moral thinking evolves alongside human knowledge, seems to have succeeded.

Today, I believe that humanity is at a critical crossroads. The radical advances that took place in neuroscience and particularly in genetics toward the end of the 20th century have led to a new era in human history. Our knowledge of the human brain and body at the cellular and genetic level, with the consequent technological possibilities offered for genetic manipulation, has reached such a stage that the ethical challenges of these scientific advances are enormous. It is all too evident that our moral thinking simply has not been able to keep pace with such rapid progress in our acquisition of knowledge and power.

Yet the ramifications of these new findings and their applications are so far-reaching that they relate to the very conception of human nature and the preservation of the human species. So, it is no longer adequate to adopt the view that our responsibility as a society is to simply further scientific knowledge and enhance technological power, and that the choice of what to do with this knowledge and power should be left in the hands of the individual.

We must find a way of bringing fundamental humanitarian and ethical considerations to bear upon the direction of scientific development, especially in the life sciences. By invoking fundamental ethical principles, I am not advocating a fusion of religious ethics and scientific inquiry. Rather, I am speaking of what I call "secular ethics" that embrace the key ethical principles, such as compassion, tolerance, a sense of caring, consideration of others, and the responsible use of knowledge and power—principles that transcend the barriers between religious believers and nonbelievers, and followers of this religion or that religion. I personally like to imagine all human activities, including science, as individual fingers of a palm: So long as each of these fingers is connected with the palm of basic human empathy and altruism, they will continue to serve the well-being of humanity.

We are truly living in one world. The modern economy, electronic media, international tourism, as well as the environmental problems, all remind us on a daily basis how deeply interconnected the world has become today. Scientific communities play a vitally important role in this interconnected world. For whatever historical reasons, today the scientists enjoy great respect and trust within society, much more so than my own discipline of philosophy and religion. I appeal to scientists to bring into their professional work the dictates of the fundamental ethical principles we all share as human beings.

❦

✤ ACKNOWLEDGMENTS ✤

I am deeply grateful to His Holiness The Dalai Lama for suffering a "chela" (student) as unworthy and undeserving as myself for some three decades, with great patience and transforming affection. He has, with great compassion, gently encouraged and supported my efforts to understand the Dharma. Editing and putting this book together has been one such project—a profound learning experience for me. Its shortcomings are entirely mine.

The Foundation for Universal Responsibility and I are deeply grateful to Ven Lhakdor, both in his incarnation as the Director of the Library of Tibetan Works and Archives, and as the Administrator of the rights to The Library of Tibet for permission to use extracts from the publications of both these institutions; and the Office of His Holiness and its now-former Secretary Mr. Tenzin Geyche for his help and support in securing and granting permission to use a number of other extracts. Mr. Chhime R. Chhoekyapa (Secretary), Mr. Tenzin Takhla (Joint Secretary), and Mr. Tempsa Tsering (Minister and Representative in Delhi) have continued to be generous with their time, wisdom, and support.

My Tibetan family of Tendzin Choegyal and Rinchen Khando have for long years been a source of great, often indulgent, encouragement.

Hay House has been a wonderful, patient, and most encouraging publisher. I am truly grateful to Ashok Chopra for reaching out to me and encouraging me to expand my universe as a writer with a number of books now in the pipeline. Ratika Kapur, my editor at Hay House, has an attention for detail and spotting obscure missing links that is rare.

Several people helped with the manuscript as it evolved, offering invaluable insights and suggestions. My gratitude to Swati Chopra, Shalini Srinivas, Jasjeet Purewal, and Bindu Badshah.

The staff at the Foundation, in particular, Kunjo Tashi, Raji Ramanan, Thupten Tsewang, and R. Lalita, have been ever present with a helping hand. Padmini and Krishnan of Kripa Consultants and my colleagues at the Public Service Broadcasting Trust,

Tulika Srivastava, Ridhima Mehra, Sohni Ralia Ram, Aarti Narain, and Sunil Srivastava, have taken on much of my everyday work obligations to create the time and space for efforts such as this.

My wife and ever my best friend, Meenakshi Gopinath; my father, Har Narain Mehrotra, and late mother, Shanti Mehrotra; and Sarada Gopinath have taught me much about the Dharma without any formal study of it themselves.

— **Rajiv Mehrotra**
Trustee and Secretary
Foundation for Universal Responsibility of
H.H. The Dalai Lama, New Delhi
www.furhhdl.org

COPYRIGHT ACKNOWLEDGMENTS

THE FOUNDATION FOR UNIVERSAL RESPONSIBILITY

"To meet the challenges of our times, I believe that humanity must develop a greater sense of universal responsibility. Each of us must learn to work not just for our own individual self, family, or nation, but for the benefit of all mankind. Today we are so interdependent, so closely interconnected with each other, that without a sense of universal responsibility, a feeling of universal brotherhood and sisterhood, and an understanding and belief that we really are a part of one big human family, we cannot hope to overcome the dangers to our very existence, let alone bring about peace and happiness."

— His Holiness The Dalai Lama

Mission

- To promote universal responsibility in a manner that respects difference and encourages a diversity of beliefs and practices

- To build a global ethic of nonviolence, coexistence, gender equity, and peace by facilitating processes of personal and social change

- To enrich educational paradigms that tap the transformative potential of the human mind

About the Foundation

The Foundation for Universal Responsibility of His Holiness The Dalai Lama is a not-for-profit, non-sectarian, nondenominational organization established with the Nobel Peace Prize awarded to His Holiness in 1989. In the spirit of the charter of the United Nations, the Foundation brings together men and women of different faiths, professions, and nationalities, through a range of initiatives and mutually sustaining collaborations. The work of the Foundation is global in its reach and transcends nationalist political agendas.

"This Foundation will implement projects to benefit people everywhere, focusing especially on assisting nonviolent methods, on improving communications between religion and science, on securing human rights and democratic freedoms, and on conserving and restoring our precious Mother Earth."

— His Holiness The Dalai Lama

The Vision

- Foster the celebration of diversity; the spirit of universal responsibility; and the understanding of interdependence across faiths, creeds, and religions.

- Support personal transformation in ways that facilitate larger processes of social change.

- Develop and sustain peace-building and coexistence initiatives in regions of violent conflict and social unrest.

- Encourage and cultivate *Ahimsa* (nonviolence) as a guiding principle for interaction among human beings and with their environments.

- Offer inclusive and holistic paradigms of education that prioritize experiential learning, cross-cultural dialogue, and a global ethic of peace and justice.

- Build the capacity for conflict transformation, human rights, and democratic freedom through partnerships with civil society groups across the globe.

- Explore new frontiers for understanding of the mind by building bridges between science and spirituality.

- Support the professional development of future leaders and decision makers through scholarships and fellowships.

- Create media products and educational materials that promote the objectives of the Foundation.

ABOUT THE DALAI LAMA

His Holiness the 14th Dalai Lama (Tenzin Gyatso) is both the head of state and the spiritual leader of Tibet. He was born on July 6, 1935, in Taktser, Amdo, in northeastern Tibet. At the age of two, the child was recognized as the reincarnation of the 13th Dalai Lama.

In 1950, at the age of 16, His Holiness was called upon to assume full political power after China's invasion of Tibet in 1949. Finally, in 1959, with the brutal suppression of the Tibetan national uprising in Lhasa by Chinese troops, His Holiness was forced to escape into exile. Since then he has been living in Dharamsala, northern India, the seat of the Tibetan political administration.

In 1989, he was awarded the Nobel Peace Prize for his nonviolent struggle for the liberation of Tibet. He has consistently advocated policies of nonviolence, even in the face of extreme aggression. He also became the first Nobel laureate to be recognized for his concern for global environmental problems.

His Holiness has traveled to more than 70 countries, spanning six continents. He has met with presidents, prime ministers, and crowned rulers of major nations. He has held dialogues with the heads of different religions and many well-known scientists.

Since 1959, His Holiness has received over 100 awards, honorary doctorates, and prizes in recognition of his message of peace, nonviolence, interreligious understanding, universal responsibility, and compassion. He has also authored more than 75 books.

❦

Lightning Source UK Ltd.
Milton Keynes UK
UKOW04f2058290115

245380UK00001B/1/P